Leslie Linsley's

High-Style, Low-Cost Decorating Ideas

Also by Leslie Linsley

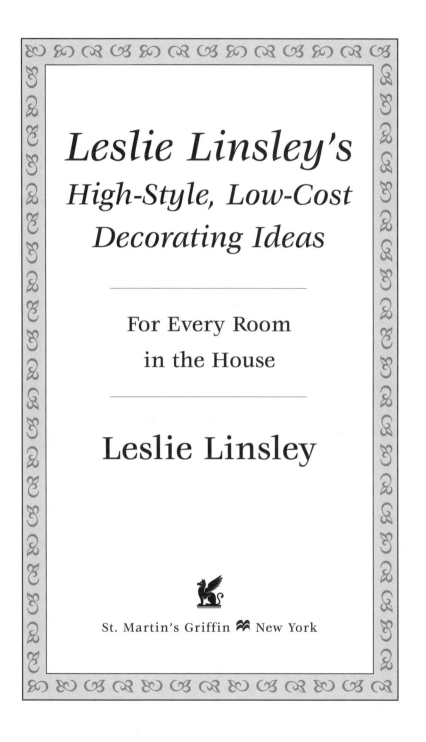

Leslie Linsley's
High-Style, Low-Cost Decorating Ideas

For Every Room
in the House

Leslie Linsley

St. Martin's Griffin ❧ New York

Library of Congress Cataloging-in-Publication Data

Linsley, Leslie.
    [High-style, low-cost decorating ideas]
    Leslie Linsley's high-style, low-cost decorating ideas : for every room in the house / Leslie Linsley. —1st ed.
      p. cm.
    ISBN 0-312-19908-2
    1. House furnishings. 2. Interior decoration. I. Title.
  TX311.L56   1999
747—dc21   99-26230
                                                      CIP

First St. Martin's Griffin Edition: July 1999

10 9 8 7 6 5 4 3 2 1

Contents

Leslie Linsley's

High-Style, Low-Cost Decorating Ideas

Introduction

Anyone can decorate on an unlimited budget. But few among us have this luxury. Decorators, artists, and designers have always come up with innovative ideas for interior decoration. The difference between them and the rest of the world is that they have the confidence to improvise. The most creative and interesting rooms are those in which the owners have a flair for using everyday objects in unexpected ways. "Style has little to do with money," said the late White House decorator Mark Hampton. "The most interesting rooms are those furnished with an eclectic mix of objects. It's a matter of looking at things in a fresh way and putting them together imaginatively."

When it comes to decorating, matching sets are outdated. Clever, comfortable, and carefree are the operative words, and the price is right. Never before have there been so many well-designed, inexpensive products for turning a home into a personal haven.

This book is about solving decorating problems using clever alternatives to buying expensive furnishings. It will turn you on to the concept of decorating with objects found at yard sales, flea markets, thrift shops, antique shops, discount stores, and ready-to-finish furniture stores, as well as to the many innovative ways in which you can use what you already have. You will also find out how easy it is to decoratively paint your walls, faux finish a piece of furniture, and add interest using fabric or wallpaper. Turning plain into interesting is just a matter of looking at things differently. Once you get started you'll find that bargain hunting and do-it-yourself makeovers can become downright addictive and lots of fun.

Today's way of decorating is about getting good value when making purchases for every room in the house. This can sometimes mean finding alternative solutions that don't cost much. For example, most people think that a living room must have a sofa. There are alternatives that can be just as comfortable and stylish. And if you happen to have a cast-off sofa bed and can't afford to replace it or cover it with slipcovers, there are clever ways to make it look better for very little money.

Furnishing a home involves lots of decisions. What should I put on the windows for privacy and good looks? Should it be blinds, curtains, shutters, or draperies? Where do I find it? How much will it cost and is there an alternative to spending a lot of money? What gives a room personality? You'll learn the answers to these questions and much more, including how to put together an interesting collection of accessories without breaking the bank. Even artwork for your walls can be accessible and affordable.

This book will tell you how to give your home much more personality when you discover how to substitute creative solutions that don't happen to cost a lot of money. You'll learn how and where to find classic, well-designed products that have stood the test of time. You'll learn how to look for practical, well-functioning products that deliver what they promise, and when you can't afford the real thing, you'll find out where to get copies of the more expensive items that function and look just as good.

Making a plan, finding inspiration, and becoming savvy about what to buy is easier than you might think. With a few helpful hints, anyone can determine what he or she likes, what's needed, what's most important, and how to put it all together to create an interesting home hassle-free and always with an eye toward saving money.

ℰ Begin with the Basics

Before you get started decorating, deal with the basics. Take stock of house and home and do all the things you've put off, like painting the bathroom or patching cracks in the ceiling. Keeping your home freshly painted, with everything in good working order, is the least expensive way to make it look up-to-date.

Getting Organized

Begin by making a list of everything you've been meaning to do, would like to do, or think you should do. Next, list everything that really screams out for attention. It might be as insignificant as cleaning out a dresser drawer and as important as having the chimney cleaned. Then attach a guesstimate of time to each item on the list, such as "a morning," "two hours," "a weekend," "a half hour." Make another list that groups together the items that will take the same amount of time. And finally, make a list of each item in each list in order of importance.

Making a Personal Plan

You can begin to create a personal plan for getting everything inside done by the time spring beckons you outdoors. For example, you might like to spend a few minutes here and there over a period of weeks sorting out dresser drawers. Or, combine a short and long project over one weekend. If you just have a few extra minutes or an extra hour at the end of the day you might be in the mood to tackle one of the items on your list. It will feel enormously satisfying to finish a task, such as hanging a new curtain in the kitchen. It does not take a lot of time, but perhaps you'd been meaning to do it for a long time. Everything eventually comes to the top of the list and what doesn't, wasn't meant to be. I like to keep a very short list and refine it daily. In this way I'm more apt to achieve success. Here's my list:

1. Put away sewing supplies
2. Clean studio
3. Decide once and for all if I'm going to reupholster the frame chair I got at a yard sale (three years ago!)
4. Organize my desk
5. Throw away enough excess junk to create one more drawer or shelf in the kitchen

If I just do the above I'll feel quite satisfied and ready to make a new list.

Making Resolutions

If a night table needs refinishing, resolve to strip the finish off and live with it for awhile until you're in the mood to stain, paint, pickle, or stencil it. Who knows, you might love it in the raw. Sometimes when I don't rush to finish something, a new solution reveals itself and often turns out to be a lot better than the original plan.

Finding More Space

Americans want a refuge that's as warm, friendly, efficient, organized, and hardworking as they are. In order to be more organized, people need to increase their storage space and that's where custom built-ins come into play. However, there are many units that give the appearance of custom built-ins and can be had for a lot less. For example, a friend of mine used a custom closet outfit to help her design a pantry off her kitchen for optimum storage. It cost about half what it would have had she hired a carpenter to do the job. Look around for preexisting storage units to solve specific problems.

Make Each Piece Work for You

Keep in mind that lots of furniture has more than one use. A trunk, for example, used as an end or coffee table can hold extra blankets, linens, or boots. If a storage item is to be used in this way, you'll want to look for one that is good-looking, not just utilitarian. Some unfinished furniture is excellent if you'd like to do some handcrafting in order to have an interesting and unusual piece in the room. More about this later in the book.

Details

Detailing within the home has become very important. Customizing means getting it right, exactly the way you want it. Adding architectural details, like molding or a wallpaper border around rooms, is an easy and inexpensive way to improve the look of your home if all the major repairs are in order.

Kitchen Re-Do

For some, it might be time for a kitchen remodeling job. A decorator who specializes in kitchen designs says that people want quality in their kitchens and this means wood in which you can see the grain. No more lacquered laminates; instead homeowners want naturally stained maple and cherry. Mixing species is becoming more popular, too. People love a hardwood kitchen floor and cabinetry made from a different wood. It's a great look. However this can be costly. But there is an alternative way to get the look.

Georgia-Pacific suggests doing over a room with their prefinished real wood paneling and they offer everything from barn plank to oak through most lumber yards.

ℬ Design Inspiration

Where does one go for inspiration when trying to redecorate a home or when moving into a new home? There are many sources; among them are magazines on just about every subject related to the home. You can even find magazines devoted strictly to one small area of the home such as bathrooms or kitchens. There is also an abundance of lavishly produced style books that tell you everything from what color to paint your walls to how to decorate with junk. There are also books on details from tiles to flooring. There's a new wave in travel books. These are full-color picture books that present the style of a particular country or place, and they provide wonderful inspiration for decorating. There is absolutely something for everyone.

European Influence

The style books about European countries are quite popular. You'll find a wide selection of books on Italian style, two new books on living the good life in Sweden, and one of my favorites, *French Country Style* (I like it because I can imagine actually using some of its ideas). If you want to create the look of an English country cottage or a room that might be found in a home in Norway, Portugal, Istanbul, or Ireland there's a book on that and any other country you can name.

Books from the Popular Magazines

The popular decorating magazines have been making good secondary use of all those magnificent photographs that appear month after month by turning to book publishing. If you aren't a regular subscriber to *House Beautiful* or *Country Living* these books will seem fresh and new. They have volumes that focus on details such as slipcovers and those that focus on decorating a weekend home. Occasionally these decorating magazines bring out a book that presents the best-designed rooms from today's leading designers.

For the Do-It-Yourselfer

My book store sources tell me there is a big market in books on faux finishing, soft furnishings, and solving specific decorating problems. If, for example, you're focused on fireplaces, you can find a general book about fireplaces and even more specifically, a book about period fireplaces. There are books on subjects like tile that show different styles, and others that show you how to lay your own tile. These types of books offer invaluable guidance for selecting materials, and good advice for how to do it.

Aside from books, there are how-to videos for all sorts of do-it-yourself home projects ranging from hanging wallpaper to refinishing furniture. On-line services, toll-free hot-line numbers, and free booklets from home centers where materials are sold provide more help. It couldn't be easier to make your home beautiful and to save money by doing some of the work yourself. In this way you can spend money on the things that you really want but can't make—a good sofa, for example.

All in the Details

When it comes to accessorizing, there are many books on details. For example, should you want to learn how to set a beautiful table there's a book that shows every kind of table setting, from a formal dinner party to a cozy breakfast. You'll learn all you need to know about carpets and rugs in a book that offers a grand survey of possibilities from the world over. Lighting, closets, kitchens for cooks, and other good, straightforward informational-style books help with the most common situations.

Eclectic Style

If what you're after is some off-the-beaten-path inspiration, you'll be happy to discover an abundance of books about decorating with junk, or flea market finds from here and abroad.

If you're an aspiring writer or artist, you can even find books that show how other creative people live and the environments in which they find inspiration.

Inspired by the Pros

On the other hand, you might be most inspired by reading about the creative people that over the years most influenced interior style. There are several books that are wonderful personal accounts by this country's best-known designers and interior decorators, people who have contributed much to American style.

Paint Resources

Concentrating on color, fabric, and paint, you'll find pretty rooms and sensible advice from books put out by such well-known companies as Laura Ashley. If painting furniture is your thing, there is a wealth of information in books for creative paint finishes.

However, anyone who has tried to pick a paint color for their walls knows that even if the intent is to go with an all-white color scheme, the choices are daunting. It is virtually impossible to choose the right shade of color the first time around. My advice: Buy the book *Color* by Kaufman and Dahl. This is not a new book, but it has become a classic and should never go out of print. When it comes to painting your rooms, you must buy this book before you even look at one paint chip. It will change the way you think about color forever.

Casual Style

If you want to decorate in a way that doesn't seem contrived, there are books for casual decorating. Home style stores with innovative approaches have cropped up all over the country and their originators often write style books that have an impact on the design world. For example, Zona is the distinctive home and lifestyle store that when it opened in Soho in New York City several years ago, with its Southwestern style, seemed utterly out of place and at once new, exciting, and somehow "right." Southwestern style often draws on the environment. Examples of this can be seen in *Zona Home: Essential Designs for Living*'s two hundred photographs with good advice offered in the text.

Another such book is *Shabby Chic,* which is about carefree, comfortable, and casual decorating. It's a great style, especially if you like nice things but your household includes little children. This style started in California, if this gives you a clue.

What's My Style

If you haven't yet figured out what your style is, there is a big interest in the Eastern philosophy of decorating called Feng Shui. The idea is to help you achieve inner peace through knowing which side of the room to place your bed on and what it means when your desk isn't facing east. These are among other interesting questions of room arrangement and decoration found in books on this subject.

❦ House and Garden Tours

More people are interested in and enlightened about style and interior design than ever before. Some are very definite about what they like; others aren't sure, but are open-minded about trying new directions in decorating. Everyone is curious about how other people decorate. This accounts for the popularity of the house and garden tours that are blossoming all over the country, especially in resort or historic towns. They offer a wonderful opportunity to see a variety of decorating styles, to get ideas for adapting in your own home, and to broaden your awareness of the use of colors, furniture styles and arrangements, arts and crafts, collections, and garden design.

How Houses Are Selected

House and garden tours have proved to be a successful way to raise money for charitable organizations. All across America, but especially in fashionable areas, a group of houses that is deemed special is chosen and opened to the public for one day of viewing. They have a certain cachet that makes them appealing, interesting, and often inspiring because of their architecture and the way they are decorated. House touring has become popular because it provides entrée into houses and gardens one might never be able to see otherwise. This is a great way to get ideas for decorating your house and to see how people with taste approach a particular decorating problem.

What to Look For

A friend of mine always goes to house tours when she's visiting other places as well as near home. I asked her what attracts her to them. "I go because I always find ideas. It might be a simple, clever way to arrange a closet, or a unique color combination, but they always spark my imagination." Since she's just bought a new home she's also interested in how the gardens are arranged and planted in her area. "It's fun to see what grows here, how the flowers are planted in relation to color. I like to see both formal and casual approaches to gardening and I'm especially curious about how a garden relates to the house and how it fits in with the rest of the landscape," she says.

Ideas from Other Parts of the Country

Whenever I visit another part of the country and there's a house and garden tour I take advantage of this opportunity. I see things I don't see at home. On Nantucket, homeowners are rather dedicated to designing their houses and gardens to reflect the island. We buy a great deal of our furnishings, accessories, and art locally. Our local farms sell indigenous plants and so everything is done in a rather integrated fashion. We're influenced by our surroundings and, for the most part, enlightened about the environment. Knowing that interior decorating decisions take into account the exterior surroundings that are so much a part of the way we live, I look for how others have intermingled indoor and outdoor areas. For example, I've been on several house tours in Key West, Florida, where decorating is related to the outdoors and a more casual approach to living. It can be a lot of fun to make a house and garden part of your travel plans.

Diversity Is Fascinating

House tours offer you the chance to see a diversity of architectural as well as decorating styles. Within a couple of hours you will surely come away with a head full of ideas for making your own houses and gardens more interesting, exciting, and personal. If you're like me, the only problem you may encounter is that when you get home you'll want to get rid of everything and start all over again!

Show Houses for Inspiration

Show houses decorated by top designers provide another excellent source of inspiration for your own decorating. The rooms often highlight the skill of the interior design professional at solving the common design problems that many of us experience. Very often the decorators redo an unsightly or old house by revamping each room to suit specific lifestyles. These show-house events usually occur in major cities and if there isn't one near your home, very often a national magazine like *House Beautiful* or *Metropolitan Home* will present the finished rooms in a special edition. Watch for these, usually in spring or summer issues.

ಔ Good Design for Less

While looking through catalogs from places like Pier 1, Crate &
Barrel, and Pottery Barn, I am impressed with the well-designed,
affordable home furnishings they offer. One can always find an
inexpensive copy of an expensive item. And then, if one digs further, a really cheap version of the knockoff. Most of these places
turn that familiar axiom around and manage to achieve the goal of
form followed by function. At first glance there's some pretty good-
looking stuff around.

Sometimes the inexpensive copies are made as cheaply as the
price suggests. However, if you're a savvy buyer you can find inexpensive, well-designed accessories to mix in with better-quality
items for effect.

I'm not recommending cheap products. I'm simply pointing
out that good design prevails and it will be copied, sometimes forever. So, whatever your needs or pocketbook, you can furnish your
home or just a niche—to look good, function well, and often last
until you can replace it with better quality.

Temporary Furnishings

There are some areas of home furnishing where you can justify
not spending a lot. The nursery is one and an area for a home office
is another. These are more or less temporary spaces. They should
function well, but they may not be permanent. A vacation house
that you use occasionally or rent out most of the time might be furnished chicly and cheaply from affordable catalogs.

Design on a Budget

It's not very difficult to create a pleasing home when money is
no object. However, designing on a budget has always been more
challenging and, I find, more interesting. Given budget restraints
and a modicum of good taste, it gets harder to come up with clever
ideas and innovative solutions to decorating problems. This chal-

lenge is what turns me on, and once you get the hang of it you'll find it most satisfying as well.

Catalog Shopping

If you want to create an interesting home office, you can do it down to the desk set without leaving home. Catalogs like *Hold Everything* and *The Container Store* offer a nice variety of accessories and good-looking functional furniture. Office-supply catalogs like those from Staples also make it easy to create functional work spaces stylishly.

I don't know about you, but I get rattled in stores when I'm faced with the many choices and decisions involved in spending hundreds of dollars. Taking the time to measure properly and to compare those measurements with pictures of items seems easier than looking at the real thing. On top of this, the choices are limited to the best for the least in each category, which is manageable.

Parson's Tables

Does anyone remember the original Parson's table? This was a square table with square legs and it came in different sizes and heights. Designed in the fifties by a teacher at the Parson's School of Design, it was sturdy and versatile and at the time, quite modern. It has never gone out of style, although it's difficult to find the original version anymore. Now one finds copies in every color and material. Home centers and five-and-tens even sell a plastic version for $3.95. Good design does last.

Desk Lamps

The other day a friend and I were singing the praises of the old gooseneck studio lamp. It comes in clamp-on and desk-top models, and the originals were sold through better art stores. Interior designers have always borrowed from other venues and this lamp ultimately found its way from the artists' studios into homes as a versatile reading lamp. It had an industrial look that was quite handsome, and it still prevails in many homes that don't have an artist in residence. Eventually knockoffs appeared, and as is the norm, they were not as sturdy, and the quality of the metal base wasn't as good. Now you can get really cheap versions that function well enough for use on a child's homework desk. But the originals still look great in a modern living room.

The Tizio Lamp

Today's version of a good work lamp is the Tizio, a high-intensity desk lamp with a swivel base that can be adjusted to nearly any angle. The original sells for around $350, but you can find all sorts of copies for under $60 and really cheap versions for under $25. There are several versions of Halogen lamps with a spring-balanced arm that are well-designed task lights. There are also copies of the copies trading several levels downward in price and function. But they are classic designs and, like tie-dyed shirts, will probably be rediscovered by the next generation as modern design.

The Banker's Lamp

Another classic that's destined to be with us forever is the banker's lamp. The green-cased glass shade with white interior was designed to reflect light back onto the work surface, and the brass base with felt cushion never needs polishing. It has an old-fashioned brass pull chain and at $45 is a terrific item that performs well and looks good. They're available through art supply catalogs and stores, and you can find the cheap version for under $20 at Kmart.

The Swing Arm Lamp

Only one lamp comes to mind when I think of lighting a bedroom, and that's the classic, swing-arm, wall lamp. It's not better looking than any other lamp, but it serves a terrific function. You can place it exactly where you need it for optimum reading in bed, it swings into whatever position you need it to be in, and best of all, it doesn't take up room on your bedside table. The originals have brass fittings and take three-way bulbs. The shades vary from silk to paper and the really inexpensive copies come in different-colored enamels as well as brass plate. The latter version isn't as sturdy as the good ones, but for a fraction of the cost, once it's secured on the wall, it works just fine.

The Utility Cart

Another item available in art stores is called a Boby utility stand. This compact classic storage unit has pivoting drawers, shelves, and wells to accommodate materials from markers to rolled papers. It glides on five casters for stability and comes in white, red, or black hard plastic. It takes up as much space as a small night table and is perfect for holding items by the changing table in a nursery; keeping sewing and art and craft supplies intact; holding all sorts of kitchen utensils; organizing bathroom essentials; organizing small tools; and as a most versatile item wherever you want to store things efficiently. The original is around $350 but you can often find them on sale for half as much and occasionally for under $100 in discount places.

Adirondack Chairs

Another well-designed item that has been around for over 150 years is the Adirondack chair. This generously sized, sturdily constructed chair with wide angled seat, wide armrests, and high back has been the furniture of choice in summer homes and on outdoor patios and porches since it was first introduced. Purists prefer it in its natural finish because it wears over time to a silvery gray color. However, you can now find all sorts of versions in a variety of colors. The copies are often smaller in size, some can be folded for easy storage (the originals could not be folded—one of their drawbacks), and they are lighter so they can be moved about for optimum sun or shade.

Director's Chairs

While we're on the subject of chairs, is there any home without a director's chair? These movie-inspired, quick and easy pull-up, occasional-seating solutions were embraced as soon as they came on the scene. They were perfect for extra seating and the strips of canvas on the seat and backrest were amazingly comfortable. The fold-up aspect made them practical as well. Now, at least three generations after they first appeared, the copies are smaller and lighter, but the frames come in all colors and the canvas seats are replaceable. Not only that, you can find the canvas in every color of the rainbow. These chairs are so reasonably priced, often as low as $10, that we don't hesitate to leave them outdoors on a deck with the full knowledge that they can be replaced, if necessary, next season.

For the Bathroom

For elegant detailing there's nothing like the heavy chrome, luxury-style, hotel bathroom accessories. If you like the look of polished chrome towel racks, bathrobe hooks, and clothes hampers you can get it in a lighter, less expensive version through places like Hold Everything. The brass hooks are plated with chrome and when they are used to hold fluffy terry robes, they will make your bathroom look and feel as luxurious as an expensive resort health spa.

Market Umbrellas

One of my favorite summertime looks for the deck is the Italian market umbrella. The canvas umbrella is supported by a wooden pole, and spokes outfitted with brass details. The canvas is available in white or deep hunter green and in two sizes. High-end catalogs like those of Smith and Hawkins have the originals for over $300, but there are less expensive versions in garden centers and through catalogs like *Pottery Barn,* and there are even cheaper versions in supermarkets and discount stores—sometimes available in more color choices as well. They're lighter and smaller, but you get the same effect for under $100.

Wicker Furniture

Good design borrowed from the past adds character to a home environment. Copies of 1920's Victorian-style wicker furniture, like chairs, tables, and love seats reminiscent of the Gatsby era, mix well with printed cushions and modern accessories for an eclectic look. Wicker is also practical because it's lightweight, durable, and water-resistant, which makes it good for indoor and outdoor use. Places like Pier 1 Imports always have a good affordable selection. Wicker picnic baskets and trunks of this type are great for small spaces, where they can do double duty as storage units and end or coffee tables. Any hardware store can cut a glass piece to fit the top. Wicker furniture is always stylish.

Classic Materials

Discover what decorators have always known: Certain inexpensive, industrial-type fabrics never go out of style. Muslin, white cotton duck, mattress ticking, chenille, and sisal are classic staples. Muslin, at under $5 a yard, comes as wide as 90–120 inches and is terrific curtain material. Sisal is a natural fiber used for floor covering. It provides a neutral background for everything else in the room.

Chinaware

If really good white chinaware from Rosenthal or Royal Doulton is beyond your budget, fret not. A set of Bauhaus dinnerware from Pottery Barn or Bistroware from Dansk is every bit as good-looking in its own right. Clean, classic lines define it and even chunky, restaurant-style dinnerware has a character that's outstanding.

Candles and Candleholders

Light your next dinner party with handblown glass lanterns and hurricane lamps holding pure white beeswax candles. No need to break the bank. Get the look of the real European candleholders from Crate & Barrel. The imported copies of these accessories are absolute winners and can only get better over the years.

Paper Lanterns

No item has prevailed longer than the ever popular Noguchi paper globe. With copies in all sizes and shapes, these inexpensive versions of the famous sculptor's original designs provide a wonderful quality of soft, romantic lighting wherever you put them.

Modular Units

Back in the sixties and seventies innovative college kids made temporary bookcases in dorm rooms by using milk crates to support strips of plywood. Free for the taking, these milk crates also proved to be perfect storage units for holding clothes, books, and any number of miscellaneous items. The modern version is designed by Rubbermaid and is called a stacking storage cube. These items are as versatile as the old ones, but they are better looking. Made of colorful, high-impact plastic, these stackable cubes are lighter in weight and make great-looking, inexpensive storage units for a child's room. They are terrific receptacles for easy pick-up of toys, or they can be used as sturdy shelf supports just as they once were. Best of all, they slide easily inside a closet to conceal mittens, hats, shoes, and other kid stuff.

℅ Decorating Dos and Don'ts

If you're on a tight budget, use your money to buy basic upholstered furniture. You can always find interesting accessories and items like wooden tables or dressers at yard sales or flea markets; these can be painted, stained, or refinished to add interest to a room. Decorators have always enjoyed the challenge of solving problems in creative ways. It might be using objects in unexpected ways, decorating small spaces dramatically, or making over a found object to look like something one might find in an expensive shop. The following ideas might be just the ticket for your decorating needs.

Dos

1. For a small space, make every piece of furniture count. Storage units should be just that—good storage space for the items you're storing.

2. Make a small bedroom look larger by using bureaus that are slightly narrow and low. Many companies make apartment-size furniture that's good for a small bedroom or dining room.

3. One large, impressive, and useful piece in a small space is often better than several small pieces.

4. When furnishing a house, buy as much as you can at one time so that everything works together. The biggest problem a novice faces when buying furnishings over a period of years is keeping the big picture in mind at all times.

5. Carefully select accessories. A vase filled with fresh flowers doesn't have to be expensive to be beautiful. And this can often look better than a table filled with small knickknacks.

6. An instant and inexpensive trick for warming up a sparse room is the placement of a group of framed family photos on one tabletop, a stack of books on a small chair or table, and a quilt or woven throw over a sofa or chair.

7. If you've just moved into your first home and can't afford artwork of the quality you'd like, decorate with framed prints. Most galleries sell limited-edition prints of the original art, and when framed beautifully, these will do the trick. A large poster or mirror on a wall can be more dramatic than a group of small prints. Framed photographs provide another inexpensive option.

8. Window treatments can be costly. There are many clever ways to soften window areas, provide privacy, and visually expand the space. Shades, wooden blinds, plain panels, valances and ready-made curtains are available for standard-size windows. When possible, use one system throughout the house. Honeycomb Duettes are perfect. Choose colors to match the walls for a continuous look. They're plain, unobtrusive, and decent looking. They can also be used under anything you add in the way of drapes.

9. Mixing inexpensive with really good elevates the inexpen-

sive items. It's also interesting to pair tables found at a yard sale and painted a funky color with a terrifically wonderful sofa.

10. Furniture usually has to do double duty in small spaces. You can cover inexpensive outdoor plastic chairs with ready-made slipcovers from a catalog and no one will be the wiser. It's a great way to throw a big sit-down party with matching chairs. And a great tablecloth will conceal just about any old table underneath.

11. All-white chinaware, no matter how inexpensive, will always look terrific. Add wonderful salad or dessert plates, each a different pattern, for interest.

12. Flowers: All one color is more dramatic than a mixed bouquet. White is elegant. For a table setting, let your napkins add the color.

13. No sideboard or buffet in the dining room? Use a serving cart. Another clever trick: If you have a file cabinet on wheels, cover it with a piece of fabric and let it double as a serving cart temporarily. Nobody will even guess.

Don'ts

1. Lots of small pieces of furniture and accessories will make a small space seem crowded.

2. Low ceilings require low pieces of furniture. A tall piece will only emphasize the low ceiling and make the room feel claustrophobic.

3. Living room end tables that don't match are more interesting than a matched set.

4. A bedroom suite is less exciting than mismatched furniture. In fact, *anything* matching is b-o-r-i-n-g!

5. A big patterned print on a sofa can be trouble, especially if there are other prints (on walls, floors, other furniture) in the room. This will create chaos, not calm.

6. Don't overdesign. There has to be some neutral background.

7. Don't think that contemporary is cold and stark-looking. It's the latest trend in decorating. The trick is to get it right, which means selecting those few pieces that click: the right size, scale, and lines. If you love clean and lean, it can even work in a tiny cottage. Think spare rather than bare.

8. Don't buy something you don't like just because it's cheap. This only adds to the clutter and depletes your resources for the things you *do* like. Plus, those cheap-but-unliked objects have a way of sticking around, never getting upgraded with a nicer model.

It's an old cliché—"buy only the things you love and the very best you can afford"—and it still sounds like pretty good advice. However, my daughter just bought a table she fell in love with. It's too big for the space where she thought it would go and it doesn't work well anywhere else. I think a smarter saying would be: "Always carry a tape measure, swatches, color chips, a floor plan for every room of the house—and don't buy anything that can't be returned easily."

ℰ Creating Comfort

The other day I was having a conversation with someone about decorating style. "Is 'country' over?" she asked. "I don't think it will ever be gone," I replied. Later I thought about this and realized that we all like country-style decorating because it represents the familiar. It adds warmth and coziness, and for those reasons it will always be with us. It is also affordable. Early folk pieces are exceptionally wonderful, easily accessible, and usually affordable. One can have a few unusual pieces such as a weathervane, a faux painted trunk, a grain scoop or crock to hold plants, or a framed embroidery sampler on the wall without breaking the bank.

Timeless Decorating

Today there is no absolute way to decorate. In fact, an eclectic mix is far more interesting than matched pieces throughout the house. Every home needs a timeless touch. One shouldn't be able to tell if the house was decorated in the 1930s or the 1990s.

Creating a Home Takes Time

There are those of us who like things to be perfect and feel that this must take as long as is necessary, whether a week or years. Others can't move into a house until it is completely furnished, for better or worse. Since it's costly to furnish a house, decisions should be made carefully. It's fun to decorate and perfect our spaces and it can be a most satisfying experience to finally find the perfect pillows or sofa to complete a room.

A friend called the other day to say she'd found the perfect dining table, though it may be a long time before she finds the chairs. A couple I know said they have been working on their living room for three years. It's almost the way they want it. They sounded a little disappointed, as if they wish the process could go on forever.

Assessing the Use of a Room

Are you getting the best use out of your rooms? Often a room can be used to better advantage depending on the season. A decorator friend switches his dining and living rooms in summer and winter.

Sometimes it's fun to create a new look with the changing of seasons. If a furniture arrangement is bothersome in any way, move the furniture around until you come up with a better arrangement. If you've been living with the same furniture for many years, buy something new to shake things up. Get rid of the one thing you've always disliked but felt you shouldn't part with because it was a relative's or it cost a lot or it's been in your life through several moves. The only good reason to keep something is because it works and you love it. Strangely, when something goes, it's easier to get a replacement than it is to get the replacement first and then remove the offensive item.

Making It Work

A house doesn't become a home until you've moved things around, removed, added, replaced, and actually lived in the space for some time. If you're just starting out, keep this in mind: Most designers strive for a classic look. Subtlety and restraint are more durable than flashiness.

Perfecting Our Need

Every time a new home catalog arrives in my mailbox I drool over the lush bedroom ensembles and routinely check off all the new bedding I want. This usually leads to a complete overhauling of my linen closet because to buy new linens means there must be room for them. In the end I pare down my desires, but this is a good way to keep perfecting the original design—by weeding out the old and adding a little at a time.

Style and Comfort Have Nothing to Do with Money

I spoke to several of my friends who are editors at decorating magazines about the future of interior design. All agree that style comes from the ability to combine old and new, traditional and modern and that cost is not a factor. Most of my friends take great pride when pointing out the one yard-sale find among the beautiful antiques or expensive fabrics they own. A careful shopper can always spot a well-designed item at a discount outlet and know how to incorporate it with everything else. In the end, what something costs is less important than how great it looks with everything else. What matters is the overall effect.

Display a Sense of Humor

Whimsy is always appreciated, and a sense of humor should be displayed somewhere in your home. The element of surprise gives a room interest. For example, use something in an unexpected way, or hang art in the bathroom, where you might not expect to find it.

Spare Doesn't Always Mean Bare

I like to edit out things that don't have meaning, look beautiful, or add to the comfort and style of my rooms. While I like a minimal look, I also like to soften things with woods, fabrics, and objects. But I try to give each object breathing room so it will be noticed. It's a good idea to remove things that don't add to your life. If it just collects dust but doesn't make you happy to look at it, pack it away for another time. It doesn't have to go forever, and this may make it easier to decide to put it away. With our lives getting busier every day, the main theme in decorating for today seems to be carefree, elegant, and spare.

Give Each Piece Its Space

When furnishing a home for the first time you might want to do it slowly. In this way you can adjust to each new item you bring into a room. Remember that each piece not only takes up the space it occupies, but the space around it as well. For example, an easy chair can be an obstacle. You need to position it where it will look best and provide the most amount of comfort, and where you can add supporting pieces as necessary to accompany the chair. If it's a reading chair you'll need a table and lamp next to it. If you buy an occasional chair to provide extra seating for a guest, it should be placed out of the way when you don't need it. But you want it to look good and enhance the rest of the room in some way. Everything you add should be both useful and good-looking. Comfort comes from many resources. Something beautiful to look at, like a vase of cut flowers, might provide comfort to the soul, while a plush, down sofa can add physical as well as visual comfort.

Familiarity Can Equal Comfort

Many people derive comfort from surrounding themselves with familiar things. For example, something you inherited from a family member will make you feel comfortable and secure when living far from your family. An old quilt inherited from a grandmother might be the perfect thing to hang on a wall, use on a bed, or place over a sofa.

Others like to decorate with framed family photographs. There's nothing like a tabletop arrangement of interesting framed photos for personalized accessories. Creating a cocoon with lots of familiar and favorite things can be the most comfortable form of decorating. If this appeals to you, make it as interesting as you can and don't be afraid to change things around as often as you like. This can be the perfect way to create warmth for winter; then remove some of your knickknacks for a temporary, sleeker look in summer.

❦ Decorating Ideas from Vacations

No matter where you go for a vacation there is always something new to find. This adds another dimension to travel. What you find doesn't have to be expensive, just different from what you might find at home. When traveling to a seaside area you might pick up a reminder of your trip, something handmade with seashells, for example. Each area of the country has its regional specialty. The important thing to keep in mind is how the item will fit in with your overall decorating style.

Travel Influences in Our Country

While visiting my sister in Arizona, we went to several art galleries where I bought two prints by an artist whose work we admired. I would like to have been able to buy an original painting, but the prints were within my budget and once home I had them framed, and they look terrific in my dining room. The Southwest colors reflect the colors of autumn in my New England environment.

Travel Influences Abroad

I've traveled often to France and I especially like the southern countryside in Provence. Each time I return I have all sorts of ideas for decorating in the French country style. Lace-edged linens washed to sheer softness have always been my passion. As luck would have it, at the well-known Sunday flea market in L'Isle-Sur-La-Sorgue, I found an armload of hand-embroidered, European-size pillowcases, table covers, and runners. This region is abundant with beautiful yellow and blue pottery, plates, flowerpots, and ceramic cooking dishes of all sizes and shapes. Provencal fabrics, also in various shades of yellow and blue, are a favorite and I brought home yards and yards to turn into pillows and table covers. Fields of yellow flowers and wild red poppies abound in spring and it's easy to see how these colors influence the Provencal decorating scheme, especially in the fabrics.

Charming Traditions

Here in America we are always looking for change in decorating style. What's coming next? What will be in style this season? In the countryside of Provence nothing changes. The style is so classic that it always seems fresh and new each time we rediscover its simple charm. And we are grateful that it stays this way. It's easy to take a bit of French style for ourselves. Lace panels cover windows, shutters and doors are painted marvelous pastel shades of lavender, pink, and faded blue. You might like to try some of these touches and make them your own.

Unstudied Casualness

The overall charm of French country style is that it seems to have just happened. It's unstudied and that's what is so appealing. Things aren't freshly painted, and a tilting shutter on a window seems to go unnoticed by the homeowner. While Americans tend to like things to be perfect, in Provence the style is more casual. Even our summer outdoor furniture must be newly painted each season, and what is broken or cracked is fixed or discarded. It's easy to accept a little unstudied casualness for a change. For example, use an old enamel coffeepot to hold a bouquet of wildflowers. Don't worry if your flower pots are slightly cracked or partially broken. Line them up on a windowsill and they'll look better than newly purchased ones. It's comforting to realize that things can look quite delightful if they are not perfect. This gives me an excuse not to paint the deck furniture every summer. Maybe the peeling paint on the window trim doesn't look so bad. Perhaps the faded slipcovers indeed make the living room sofas more inviting than new ones would. And maybe it doesn't matter that the bathroom curtains, made from a flea market table runner, don't quite fit all the way across the window. Decorating that simply happens because you've put together the things you love, or have uncovered while traveling, can offer a great deal of aesthetic pleasure.

Flea Market Finds

Yard sales, flea markets, second-hand shops and antique hideaways are where you'll find those one-of-a-kind things that can turn your house into a home. While traveling we always stop the car when we  see a sign for a *brocante* (the equivalent of a permanent yard sale, one step removed from a flea market and very far down from an "antique" shop, in the heirarchy of shopping outlets). Here is where we uncover the things discarded by French country dwellers. The anticipation of uncovering uniquely designed items made for ordinary use is most exciting; it is very similar to the element of discovery that entices us to attend yard sales at home. Buying a mixing bowl that has perhaps been in someone's family for many generations is more meaningful than finding such an item in a boutique. Seeing it on an open shelf alongside my grandmother's mixing bowl in my kitchen gives me a great deal of pleasure. This, to me, is what "decorating" is all about. By using things that have a special meaning because they remind you of someone you love, or of the experience you had finding it, adds a dimension to the environment you've created. Others simply see a tasteful and interesting arrangement of things.

Regional Influences

Sometimes traveling opens our eyes to different styles that we might find attractive. This can be an overwhelming influence and give you a decorating direction to use throughout your home. If Santa Fe style is appealing to you but you live in the Southeast, you can still create this look by incorporating the colors and furnishings to simulate the look. Bring home a few items that represent the area and work around them. It doesn't have to cost a lot to get the look.

French country influences my style, but not totally. I like the lace curtains, the casual accessories, and a smattering of the colors for my summer makeovers. This is reflected in the throw pillows on my sofa and the tableware I use outdoors. But by fall I'm ready to cozy up with an American country look that is filled with warm woods and natural colors. However, I still decorate with an eye toward casual.

When weeds grow between the bricks on my patio I hope I can remember to view this as charming instead of an annoyance. Best of all I can have the American attitude about keeping up with style changes and still take on a Provencal attitude, because yellow and blue is always pretty.

Different Style Influences for Nontravelers

You don't have to travel to Provence to find fresh decorating ideas. Now more than ever before there are books that will give you all the inspiration you'll need. And you don't have to travel far to find those items you covet for your own home. Home stores and catalogs offer everything from furniture to carpets to accessories from anywhere you can imagine. These full-color, lavishly produced style books are often referred to as dream books because they transport you to other worlds. Creating the look of another country can be a lot of fun and a lot less expensive than traveling to the place.

℘ Luxuries

What is a luxury? When I posed this question to a handful of style-makers they all answered unanimously with "time"—more time to be lazy. More time to luxuriate in a hammock with a good book, in a bubble bath without interruptions or distractions. After that there were more tangible things that represented luxury, like an exceptional meal, a pure cashmere throw, a spectacular hotel room, an expensive bottle of wine, the services of a top-notch gardener. But since we're concerned with making home a haven that is both visually and aesthetically comforting you might want to consider splurging on that one item that will create the look you're after and bring you pleasure each time you look at it.

Every Luxury Is Relative

If you think it's totally outrageous to even think about buying something so extravagant as a leather lounge chair for thousands of dollars, you might not think it's terribly unreasonable to buy chenille throw pillows to put on your old wing chair. And if you're making do with painted, ready-to-finish end tables, treating yourself to a magnificent blown glass vase might elevate the furnishings. When looking at what you have, or what you have sacrificed in the scheme of furnishing with high style for low cost, spending money on one luxury may not be out of the question.

Luxuries Worth Considering

Take a trip to your favorite shopping haunts and make a list of those items that are over the top in the luxury department. Pretend that money is no object, and you're about to treat yourself to one wonderful thing that's unique, one-of-a-kind, unnecessary in the scheme of everyday living, but indeed very special. Here are some of the items that I think of when furnishing with luxury in mind.

1. A handwoven silk and cashmere throw: You can have the shabbiest of sofas and no one will notice that it's a cast-off if this item is draped over it. Relatively speaking you get the look of a new sofa for a fraction of the cost. Choose a soft color that's as elegant as its touch.

2. A handmade dollhouse completely furnished with exact replica period furniture down to the last detail in the style you would do your house if you could afford to do so. I actually know a lady whose family bought her the dollhouse for a special birthday, and each year they chip in to buy pieces of furniture. She's had enormous pleasure furnishing her dream home, room by room. The dollhouse is on display on a sideboard in her dining room.

3. An original painting by an artist you admire. Or a piece of pottery that is exceptionally beautiful.

4. A complete set of bed linens in the highest thread count you can find. Your bed will be set for pure, luxurious lounging. Now this is talking my language. I'm a bed person. It's the place I like most to be, and the prettier and softer the bedding the happier I am. If this is your cup of tea, treat yourself to an embroidered set of sheets, shams, and duvet. One hundred percent Egyptian cotton bedding is wonderfully soft and crisp looking. You'll find it in the softest pastel colors as well as pure white.

5. Don't stop there. Why not buy a top-of-the-line mattress set? You'll have absolutely no excuse for a bad night's sleep.

6. Silk- or damask-covered, oversize pillows for accents any-where are costly. But this is one item you can actually have for a fraction of its cost in a store. Splurge on the fabric of your choice and a down-filled pillow form. Stitch it up yourself in less than an hour and you'll have exactly what you want for the cost of the materials.

7. Any authentic early American folk art such as a moveable tin toy, a weathervane, a quilt in perfect condition, or a hand-dyed McAdoo hooked rug for a luxurious touch of art underfoot. As I've stated elsewhere, these items are easy to find in reproductions if you simply want the look and can't justify spending for an original. It's often hard to tell the real from the copy. Only you will know. When it comes to buying a luxury item, however, having the real thing can be part of the satisfaction.

8. A model of an actual boat can be the perfect luxury for a col-lector. Such an accessory placed on a mantelpiece, in a bookcase, or on a table in front of a window looks sensational and can be the main attraction in a room.

9. A basket is a traditionally inexpensive item, unless it's an authentic American Indian one. The latter are exceptional, sought-after collectibles carried in specialty antique shops. There are also handmade baskets that are sculptural and are considered works of art not just utilitarian pieces. Craft shops and art galleries are where you'll find them.

10. Another luxury that might not be considered so extravagant by some is really good, fresh potpourri. European soap is another, as are silver candleholders—that come with fragrant candles—from England. My luxury is always having on hand a box of the famous Harry Turner scented votive candles. They exude the faint scents of lilacs and magnolias.

11. When I asked my daughter Amy and her husband, Stefan, what they would choose in the luxury department they both agreed. It was a set of six bone-handled steak knives made of tempered steel from the French township of Laquiole. They come in a wooden, lacquered, painted box.

12. When I asked a friend who is a wine expert what over-the-top luxury he would opt for the answer wasn't surprising, "A 1967 Chateau d'Yquem sauternes. I would venture to say you won't find that too easily." Top off your list with the luxury of the century—a case of expensive wine or champagne to keep on hand for special occasions. That should make anyone's home seem high style no matter how low cost the furnishings.

When you've made your choices, kick off your shoes, lean back against the down cushions on your European bed, casually toss the silk and cashmere throw over your legs, uncork the sauternes, and settle into the lap of luxury.

Decorating
with Color

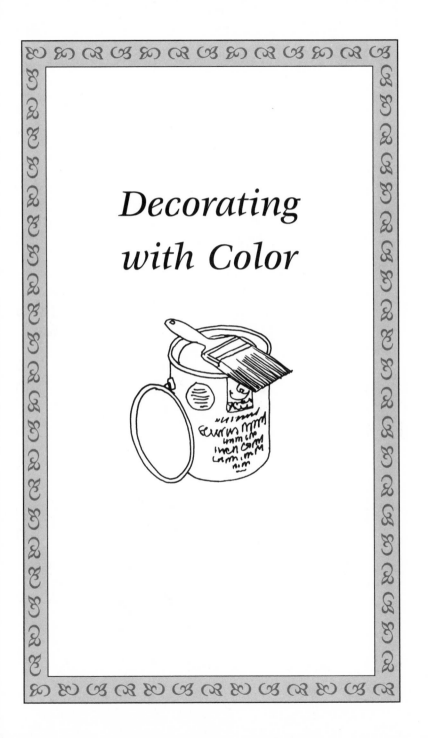

ℬ Change the Look with Color

The most striking and inexpensive way to change the look of a room and give it an up-to-date lift is with accents of color. This can mean painting the walls, adding throw pillows or colorful accessories, or adding fresh flowers and plants in bright colors. I like monochromatic rooms because it's so easy to add touches of color wherever and whenever I'm in the mood. If you start out with a shade of white paint on the walls and choose basic white or off-white furnishings, you can't go wrong.

Bright and Sunny

Every season brings with it a new color palette. Imagine rooms painted with alternating stripes of apple green and white, or persimmon and butter yellow. With these colors you can transform even the gloomiest room into one that is bright and sunny. A sunshine yellow room would do much to lift the spirits on a gray day.

What the Decorators Have to Say

When decorator Mario Buatta designs a show-house room it's usually filled with colorful fabrics in bold floral patterns that would put any garden to shame. Rainbow-striped fabrics are de rigueur this season and Buatta goes over the top with swags of silk, formalizing windows once again. He calls his new look "English country with brighter colors."

While lavender is becoming a popular color in decorating, no one used it better than designer Albert Hadley, who called it the "new beige." Teaming it with dark, dark browns and mahogany woods, this color, used for upholstery, not just accents, is rather striking. My tendency would be to use it sparingly, perhaps on throw pillows or the upholstery on dining room chairs. I'm not so confident as to suggest sofa and chairs in shades of purple.

Wallpaper Wisdom

Busy, patterned wallpaper is once again in style. Used on bedroom walls it's more suited to large rooms and balanced with large pieces of furniture such as an ornate armoire and four-poster bed.

A Citrus Mix

In southern climates we've always found daring mixes of citrus colors that are warm and exciting at the same time. Painted furniture and colorful quilts are part of this scheme and just as these items work with our country homes, they warm up a modern environment as well. Exuberantly colorful fabrics and finishes can be used in rooms of every style.

Ice Cream Shades

Never before have so many shades of pastel ice cream colors like pistachio and strawberry been used on everything, even wooden furniture. It's a refreshing look that's easy and inexpensive to achieve. When a new color palette hits the scene, I simply buy a small item such as a vase, cover a throw pillow, or repaint a yard-sale find in one of the new colors in order to keep my home looking fresh.

White Is Always Right

When all is said and done, I still favor shades of white and even if I don't get to it for two more years, I fully intend to create my all-white rooms even if it's out of style and chartreuse is totally cool. I once made the statement, "Totally cool grandparents don't have white sofas." I should have added, "Unless the furniture is covered with machine-washable slipcovers."

Got the Blues?

Many people carry swatches of their fabric with them. Others carry paint samples. This is an excellent idea when shopping for home accessories. For example, blue is probably the most popular home decor color. However, there are many different hues and shades of blue and it's extremely difficult to remember colors. Also, when shopping for a pillow you might find one in a shade of blue and think it will go well with the other blue colors in the room. But not all blues work well together.

The blue fabrics that I bought in Provence have a little bit of purple in them and the blues are closest to periwinkle. Then there is hydrangea blue which also has some purple tones. But there are true blues and pale blues and iris and morning glory and an enormous variety of other shades. When in doubt it's much better to introduce another, complementary color like yellow or green, rather than try to match blues. However, it can be incredibly interesting to mix different patterns of blue prints in a pile of pillows on a sofa. Or, mix dark and light blue shades throughout the house. Used in this way the difference in blue colors is not so crucial and in fact can be quite interesting.

∞ Warm to White

Most decorators I know live in neutral rooms. This is because they often work with color and patterns all day and need the comfort that a monochromatic room offers. However, a white room doesn't have to be as stark as a hospital room. In fact, shades of white combined with natural textures can be warm and inviting and at the same time very serene. If you want a high-style look for minimal cost, painting everything white is the best way to start.

White Is Stylish

An all-white color scheme works in any style home; modern, traditional, even historic. Interior designer Vincente Wolfe says,

"Shades of white make a home gracious and restrained, restful and open, elegant and comfortable."

Shabby Chic

The trick with white is to keep things a bit loose so the room doesn't become too formal and uptight. Slouchy slipcovers and oversized soft pillows work for the sofa. I prefer simple pillows that are made of cotton, chintz, or linen and have only crisp piping or no decorative touches at all. Sisal rugs are good floor covers. Large baskets holding pots of fresh herbs are more casual than formal floral arrangements.

Different Shades of White

White is an interesting color (or noncolor) because it changes with the light of day. Sometimes it can look creamy and other times gray, depending on the time of day and whether or not the sun is shining, as well as the location in the house.

Neatness Counts

It's not easy to live in an all-white home. When it's messy it seems even messier. When there are newspapers, books, mail, and the normal pieces of everyday living about, it is more jarring than when these items are absorbed into a room filled with color and pattern. So, if you can't imagine a place for everything and everything in its place you'll probably want to add color and patterns here and there.

Adding Color

It's easier to add color to an all-white room than to start with paint colors and be confined to decorating within that color scheme. People often tell me their color scheme and then complain that they're having trouble buying a single pillow because the blue isn't exactly right. If you introduce color, mix up the shades just as you would with neutrals. It's more interesting, for example, to use a variety of different shades of rose than to have everything match perfectly. In fact, using different shades of one color and introducing just one accent color, such as deep green or purple to a rose and white room can create a wonderful look.

The Naturals

If you like the monochromatic look, use a lot of colors from nature. For example, taupe, leafy green, goldenrod, terra-cotta, sunset red, and earth tones will be wonderful accents in an off-white room.

Add Warmth to a White Room

Add warmth to a white room with works of art. This doesn't have to be just paintings, but handcrafted objects as well. A brightly colored glass bowl, for example, will make a bold statement on a wooden table in a white room.

Color in Small Doses

The thing you don't want to do is invest in an object that's expensive and large, such as a boldly patterned sofa or carpet that you might tire of very quickly. It's so easy to add color to a room in small doses to see what works best for you and the room and how it relates to the rest of the house. A little color in a white room can make a strong statement, so choose your colorful objects carefully. Something as simple as a bookcase can add interest, texture, and color to a white room. Remember, woods add warmth.

Lighting

Lighting is another way to bring warmth into a minimal room. Use low lighting in the form of table lamps rather than recessed lighting, and use rheostats for lighting control.

White Bedrooms

In my opinion there is no other color for a bedroom. It's restful and calming and appeals to the senses. This year I bought a linen duvet of grayish beige and white checks. I added lighter-checked accent pillows and this is what I will use for fall and winter. In the summer it's all white. Moving toward the different textures and shades will make the room warmer after the stark cool look of summer. Using white as a base allows me to have this comfortable versatility.

The Collector's Dilemma

It's hard to keep things uncrowded and uncluttered when you love collecting. A decorator I know lives in a tiny cottage filled to brimming with the things she loves, yet it seems spacious because it is devoid of color. The living room, kitchen, dining room, and bedrooms share the same decorating elements. Creamware pottery lines kitchen shelves, and every tabletop is filled with interesting collections, but everything is in shades of white, gray, beige, and cream, with a few silver objects. She uses baskets, straw, vintage linens, rich old wood, crocheted pieces, lots of books, fresh greens, and candles. Again, white walls create the perfect backdrop for all this wonderful variety.

℘ Seeing Red!

There are two times in the year, Christmas and Valentine's Day, when red becomes the dominant color displayed in shop windows and magazines. For such an uplifting color, it's highly undervalued as a base around which to build your decorating scheme.

The Pros and Cons of Red

My usual advice is, when in doubt paint it white. However, lately I've uncovered some smashing rooms done in shades of red. Here's what one of my favorite decorating gurus, Mark Hampton, said about red: "Everyone loves red. It is the happiest of colors. Red is a symbol of easy playfulness and it broadcasts vigor."

There are however, many prejudices voiced against red rooms in a home, including:

1. It only belongs in a child's room.
2. It belongs in public places, such as the carpet in a hotel or lounge of an airport.
3. It's too priestly or Victorian.
4. It's reminiscent of old-time saloons with crimson flocked wallpaper.
5. It's too regal, as in red velvet capes.

Prejudices aside, red offers marvelous possibilities and is becoming more and more popular.

Love It or Lose It

The second house I ever owned, many houses ago, had a large dining room that I painted tomato red. It was a bold move back then and the results were quite dramatic. The room was always bright and felt cheerful even on a gloomy day. Many years later I met the couple who were still living there and they told me it took ten coats of white to cover the red walls and even then, when the sun filled the room it had a pink cast. The moral: If you paint a room red, be sure what you really want is a strong dominant color. This is a hard mistake to cover up.

The Best Places for Red

Where is red most effective? Hallways look terrific in red. Most entryways are dark, and red is an excellent color for creating excitement in dark areas. Rather than just brightening as with a light color, red invites warmth and richness. Red also works well with many other colors. I've used it in my white rooms with dark hunter green.

Red is a wonderful color for a dining room. Food, people, and flowers look good in a red room. Red positively makes a room glow when there is candlelight or a fire in the fireplace. Red enhances all the elements in a library or den. Books, dark wooden furniture, tapestry, needlework, leather, and brass look good against red. Bright white is an excellent companion for your wood trim and doors. Red paint or wallpaper is elegant inside bookcases or a china cabinet. Oriental rugs with red in them are a good choice for floor covering in a red room. Red is ravishing with bronze or gold leaf. Red upholstered fabric is wonderful with dark mahogany furniture.

A Decorator Has the Last Word

The late decorator Billy Baldwin is best known for his monochromatic rooms. However, he was also a master at using red and dark green skillfully. He designed many red rooms for such famous clients as Diana Vreeland. And remember, paint is the cheapest way to transform a room, so why not a rich red?

Red furniture?

You might think it sounds horrible until you think of Chinese red-lacquered furniture. I have a red-painted occasional table and it seems to fit in wherever I put it. Sometimes it holds a red tole lamp and at other times a large white vase of red or white roses with deep green leaves.

Shades of Red

Of course there are many different shades of red. Some lean toward the pink red of brick or terra-cotta, others have blue or purple in the color. Then there are the clarets. Each shade creates different atmospheres. Dark cranberry red is often found in early New England houses. Used with deep green or federal blue you have a perfect Early American mix.

Paint specialists often recommend adding a clear glaze to red wall paint. This gives it a bright, rich finish. Sometimes deep red, right out of the can, appears muddy and dull after it dries. In this case, apply a coat of semigloss, clear polyurethane (nonyellowing) for the glazed effect.

Red Can Be All Wrong

Where is red all wrong? Have you ever seen a red bedroom or kitchen? Probably not too often. This is because red is not particularly restful for a bedroom nor does it work well with morning light. It is really a mood enhancer when you want to create an air of romance, coziness, elegance, or excitement. I guess these adjectives could apply to the bedroom. However, before painting your bedroom red, I suggest tacking a piece of red fabric to the wall opposite your bed. Wake up each morning to that color on one wall. If you still love it at the end of the week, you've got your answer.

Undoing a Mistake

A young woman came into my shop and told me she had painted her bedroom bright red. She thought it would be rich and warm, but it came out all wrong. "It screams like a fire engine siren," she admitted. "I can't stand it and I don't know how to tone it down." I stood dumbfounded for a second or two. I couldn't suggest adding a little white to the color because then she'd end up with something even worse, bubble gum pink. I thought about this for a long time. "Why not paint all the trim with glossy white," I suggested. Wrong. She had just installed a linen-colored Berber rug.

Wallpapering would be another solution, but this would have required more money and more work when what she wanted was to salvage what she could of the red room. Finally I thought the best solution might be to apply a faux finish, like a sponge treatment or ragging. If you have a red wall that's too bright, the following will tone it down: Make a mixture of equal parts eggshell gray or brown paint and glaze. When applied to the walls, let some of the red show through. My advice is this: Red is all wrong for a bedroom, no matter what shade or tone. It's simply too risky. The dining room is a good place for red if you love the color.

ℰℭ When Yellow Works

Yellow has been popping up in all sorts of unlikely places and teamed with colors you might not have thought to use it with, such as purple or lavender. Just as with white, there are many shades of yellow, and the subtleties we find in nature are just as interesting in paint colors, wallpaper, and fabric patterns.

Symbols of Spring

Daffodils are the exalted symbol of spring. There is nothing quite so cheerful after a cold winter than a mason jar filled with yellow daffodils on the kitchen counter. Suddenly everything smells better, looks fresher, and the bright yellow color is the prettiest ever.

Choose Carefully

Yellow can be a difficult color to use in decorating, especially for painting walls. This is because it can look muddy or too brash. It's important to look at different shades of paint chips before making a final decision. In fact, I usually suggest having the smallest amount of paint mixed, trying it on a large poster board, and taping this to the wall you intend to paint. Live with it for a few days to see how the natural and artificial light change the color, before making the final commitment.

Where to Use Yellow

A little bit of yellow goes a long way toward brightening a room or hallway. I once used yellow to paint the inside of a closet. Everytime I opened the closet door it was a welcome surprise. A very pale shade of yellow looks good in a kitchen or nursery. If there's any yellow color in your wallpaper, consider using yellow on the window, door, and wall trims. Look for other areas in your home to add a spot of yellow to. You'll be amazed at how fresh and delightful the addition of this color can be.

Shades of Yellow

Faded yellow paint has character. Butterscotch yellow in a shade found on early creamware and crockery would make an interesting background if used to paint a wall holding open shelves in a kitchen—for example, arrange pure white chinaware and mixing bowls with those in shades of yellow or blue. Mix with a few pieces of blue and white spatterware or blue-banded bowls.

Yellow for Warmth

Even in an all-white room, touches of yellow will warm things up. Now and then I introduce very pale yellow into my bedroom. A yellow and white fabric for throw pillows, a yellow patterned cloth on a night table, a fabric-covered headboard, pale yellow sheets and pillowcases are a few ways to introduce yellow without the major commitment of painting or wallpapering.

Accents of Yellow

Many summer porches and living rooms are decorated with a blue and white theme. This year, when you reassess your home, consider adding something yellow, such as botanical prints—to the walls, a few pieces of pottery, a vase, pillows, or a scatter rug—to liven things up.

New Life for Old Furniture

Faux painting techniques are popular for finishing country furniture. Give new life to old kitchen chairs by sponge or spatter-painting them with yellow and white paint. Chairs in almost any condition can be made to look good with either of these techniques. If the chairs are already painted, you don't have to spend hours removing the paint. Begin by sanding lightly all over to remove any flaking paint. Then coat each piece of furniture with Bin or Kilz sealer (available at paint stores). Let dry overnight. This enables you to apply paint or other finishes without removing what was already there. A word of warning: These products have an oil base and cannot be washed from hands or brush with water. Use rubber gloves when applying and a sponge brush that can be thrown away once the job is done. Cleanup must be done with mineral spirits or turpentine.

How to Sponge-Paint

Give the piece a coat of white latex paint and let dry. To sponge-paint you'll need a natural sponge (not the kind used for washing dishes), that has big crevices and is sold in paint and home centers. You'll also need rubber gloves and a small can of yellow latex paint (or acrylic in a tube). Dip the sponge into the second color and tap off the excess paint onto newspaper. Then simply pounce all over the prepainted chair. Continue to pounce the paint all over in a random pattern, leaving some areas of white here and there. The objective is to keep it subtle. The second color shouldn't be too obvious. You want to blend and soften as you continue to apply the sponge. Many novices make the mistake of thinking the two colors should contrast greatly. Sponge-painting done expertly is quite subtle and, when finished, has a softly textured, mottled appearance. This is your goal. Stand back, look at the piece, and continue to go over it until it has that subtle, blended appearance. When finished, let dry. Then coat with a water-based varnish. If you use a polyurethane it tends to yellow the finish, and if you've used a blue paint, it can sometimes turn it green.

How to Spatter-Paint

For a spatter-paint treatment you'll need the same items as used for sponge-painting except you will substitute a toothbrush for the natural sponge. Once the background color is painted and completely dry, you will add spatters of color over all surfaces. Put a small amount of the second paint color in a shallow dish. Dip the toothbrush into the color and wipe excess paint onto newspaper. Then, while holding the brush over the piece of furniture, run your thumb over the bristles so that the paint spatters in a random manner. Continue to cover the furniture with spatter drops of paint. Finish as described above for sponge painting.

ℰℓ Using Bright Colors Successfully

Orange? You have to be kidding, I thought, as I read the reviews of the furniture show in Milan, Italy. In High Point, North Carolina, the showrooms are subdued with variations of beige. How can such a radical departure cross the ocean and insinuate itself into our homes? Add to the orange another up and coming "hot" color, chartreuse, and you have a color combination not many of us could live with. New colors are introduced each season. So how do we stay up-to-date without going crazy? Perhaps there are ways to incorporate new and sometimes radical colors into our decor in small doses.

Colorful Dining

The only place I might use orange is on a dining table. A table setting for a party might be pretty in these vivid, acid colors. Create a centerpiece by filling a bowl with bright oranges and adding a few green limes for accent. Or, you might use a bunch of plump orange/yellow peaches. In this way you can be in style without painting your dining room orange.

In all honesty, I've seen rooms painted these colors in the South and they look terrific. However, I don't think this is something I'd recommend unless you live in the tropics, where the bright light tends to wash out even eye-popping colors. Anywhere else in the country, I don't predict a run on orange paint at most home centers in the near future. Coral, perhaps, but not orange!

Cheerful Summer Party Decor

For a summertime party on the porch, fill a large clay pot with ripe nectarines or kumquats to use as a centerpiece. Or fill a bright yellow plastic watering can with anemones or daisies. Fill large colorful buckets with ice to hold bottles of soda on a side table.

Colorful Oversized Napkins

Oversize napkins are perfect for buffets or outdoor dining. These are a cinch to make from scraps of pretty and colorful printed fabrics. You'll get the look you want for pennies and a few minutes of your time.

Cut each square into pieces measuring twenty-two to twenty-three inches. Fold under ⅛ inch of the raw edges and press. Again fold back ⅛ inch and press. Stitch along hemline by hand or machine. Then fold and roll up each napkin and tie with ribbon, yarn, or raffia. Then fill a basket with the rolled napkins placed on end. They create a practical and pretty addition to your table.

Tabletop Decorations

A friend from Sweden says they often decorate a table with crushed stones or pieces of crystal. She also suggests using marbles or sea glass scattered over the table. Then place votive candles in glass containers here and there, and the light will glint off the glass.

Quick and Easy Tabletop Decor

Sprinkle a bagful of confetti in bright primary colors (orange and chartreuse perhaps) or pastels over the tabletop before adding the plates and silverware. I like to scatter shells around and arrange my votive candles in large clamshells. For a summery party, set a table with something orange to see how you like the color. A tablecloth might be nice with chartreuse napkins and orange zinnias as a centerpiece. Or scoop out the fruit from half an orange, lemon, or grapefruit and use the cups to hold votives.

Brighten Dull Colors

If the paint on your walls is too flat and you want a richer effect, it's easy to add a little zing. Apply a coat of eggshell varnish over it all. Another way to get this effect is to mix equal parts of transparent glaze with the same color paint for the second coat. High-gloss polyurethane over the painted walls will also give them luster. Test these techniques on different pieces of poster board and hang them on your wall to see how each looks. Leave them up for a few days to choose the best one.

℅ Shapes, Textures, and Colors

To spruce up any area of your rooms in a quick and easy way, simply take a new look at your accessories and rearrange them in groupings by shape, size, color, and texture. It's fun to create tabletop vignettes with decorative accessories that relate to one another in this way.

Begin with an Egg

If you haven't a clue where to begin, here's a suggestion that always works for me. Use an ordinary egg for inspiration. It's a wonderful shape, and eggs can be found in many shades of natural color. Create a still-life setting on a table using objects that are circular and oval in shape. Avoid anything with sharp edges, such as a box or  wooden frame. Be sure all the objects are eggshell colors and arrange three or four items to make up an interesting display. These items don't have to be related in any other way.

Tabletops

Use this same principle when entertaining. For example, create a dining table centerpiece. Assemble a group of fruits or vegetables in complementary shapes and colors and arrange them in a basket. Even an arrangement of different whole melons can be quite elegant. Or use eggplant, asparagus, and a variety of cabbages.

Natural Textures and Colors

I use the top of my china cabinet to display a group of accessories, which I change from time to time. My latest grouping is made up of several wooden spool candlesticks; an old-fashioned hat stand; a round grain scoop; and a large, round, rustic basket. They are all rounded in shape, of varying shades of brown, and everything is made of wood. The rough texture of the basket adds interest to the other smooth-textured items.

Learn to Edit

If you've assembled a group of items that relate in one way or another, work with them to create an arrangement. Stand back and look at what you've created. Now take one item away. Then another. Now rearrange with what you have left. Eventually you will be able to decorate with one accessory, a simple sprig of flowers in a beautiful vase, for example.

Walls and What to Put on Them

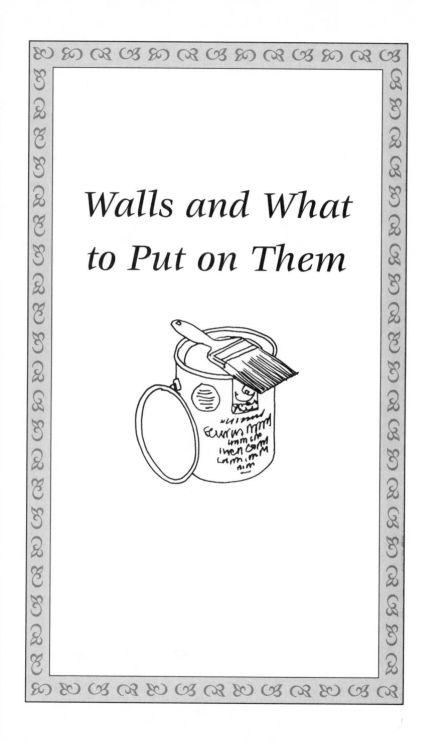

ᏚᎧ Paint Is the Cheapest Form of Flattery

Revelations can come about under the oddest circumstances. While standing in the paint aisle of Kmart it occurred to me that I don't have the patience for perfection. Martha Stewart was responsible for this revelation. Whatever she does, she expects nothing less than perfection, both from herself and others, and her taste is impeccable. As I stood there mulling over my paint options, I realized that everyone wants to be perfect at something. In this regard I decided to come up with one simple idea that anyone can do in order to achieve a moment of perfection.

When in Doubt, Paint It White

One evening, while having dinner at a friend's house I found the solution, one that might work for anyone. She had purchased a dark and dingy house in which everything was covered with dark paneling. With more time and energy than money and with the help of a few good friends she painted every square inch of that house, including the brick fireplace, with white latex paint. The before and after pictures are proof that anything is possible. The house now looks bright and modern and shows off the basic good design of the space. Paint it white and you can't go wrong. Don't know what to do with that old furniture? Paint it white!

Simple Furnishings

When you have an all-white environment it's best to keep it light. Heavy, dark furniture won't do. Add furniture of light woods and accessories such as a collection of interesting baskets on a mantelpiece. Old crocks and jugs can be interesting, even grouped in a corner on the floor. A quilt hanging on a large wall or on a stairway wall makes a dramatic accessory.

A Tip from the Pros

During a recent visit to the Sherwin Williams plant I learned that if you wipe any piece of furniture down with denatured alcohol (available in paint stores), you can then apply paint without stripping. My further advice is to make your primer coat Bin or Kilz, available in home centers. Then use a semigloss paint and you're on your way to a brighter future.

℅ Paint Tips

At our house something always needs painting. We used to buy inexpensive brushes because cleaning brushes is a thankless job. The cheap ones can be thrown out with abandon after a job is done. But anyone who paints knows that the better the tools, the better the end results.

The Better the Tools the Better the Job

Some people throw them out, others soak them for days, some even freeze paintbrushes to avoid cleaning them. The paint never seems to completely come out of the bristles, making it a painstaking process. Recently I discovered a product that has reformed me and I have begun to use better brushes because of it.

Brush Stuff Paint Brush and Roller Cover Conditioner from The Flood Company makes cleaning paintbrushes and rollers easy and fast. We use it in our studio and it's great. It's one of those products that does what it claims to do. It works with any kind of paintbrush, whether natural China bristle, nylon, or polyester, and with most any kind of paint including latex, acrylic or oil based, even quick-dry primers.

Simply apply the cream to the bristles or the roller before painting. It coats the bristles or roller fabric and prevents paint from bonding to them. When you clean up, the paint washes off easily with water for water-based paints or solvent for oil paints. Then you reapply the cream and you're ready for your next painting project. Brush Stuff doesn't affect the color or properties of the paint. The brushes were actually more pliable so the paint could be applied more easily. I think it makes the brush last longer, making it more feasible to buy better quality brushes. The six-ounce tube says it's good for one hundred applications.

Tips from the Pros

The following tips are reprinted with permission from *The Painter's Handbook, Professional Edition, 1995.*

1. When making a major color change, from dark to light, for example, use a white base coat instead of a primer. It is a common misconception that the surface should be primed, when actually a white base coat hides more effectively.

2. To establish if paint on an old piece is alkyd or latex, rub the surface with a cloth wet with nail polish remover. Latex paint will come off on the cloth. Alkyd will not be disturbed. You will then know how to remove, refinish, or repaint your piece.

3. To see what a paint color will look like in an eggshell or semigloss finish, wet the paint chip with water to avoid any surprises. Most manufacturers produce color chips in a low sheen.

4. Synthetic (nylon) brushes should not be left standing on their bristles in solvent or water. The bristles will develop a permanent curl, making the brush useless. (I use a coffee can and first make a hole in the plastic lid, then push the brush handle through the hole enough so that the bristles will be suspended in the solvent.)

5. Brushes made from natural bristles should not be used in

water-based paints. These bristles absorb water and swell, destroying the shape of the brush.

6. When using masking tape to protect a surface other than carpet, such as molding, remove the tape as soon as you can after painting. You will get a cleaner edge. For painting baseboards where there is carpet, use 2-inch masking tape around the edge of the carpet, allow about ¾ inch to lie on the baseboard, and then tuck it down over the carpet fibers as you pull them away from the baseboard. The paint tape will not stick firmly to the carpet fibers, so let the paint dry before removing the tape.

7. Use an extension pole on your roller handle. It allows you to use longer strokes and saves you from bending over to refill the roller with more paint. It also speeds up the job and makes it easier to maintain a wet edge. This is especially good when painting a ceiling.

Painting Walls

If you're in love with an unusual color, perhaps lime green or tomato red and you're thinking of painting an entire room with the color, do the following: Have your paint center mix the color in a small amount. Then buy two poster boards (approximately 20 × 30 inches) from an art supply store and paint them with the newly mixed color. Tape these boards to one of the walls you're thinking of painting. You need this much of the paint color to get the full impact. Live with the color for at least a week. If, at the end of this time you still love the color, you can buy the amount of paint needed to do the job. Also keep in mind that the color on those tiny paint chips always looks lighter than the color will look on your walls. When choosing a color it's a good idea to go one, even two shades lighter. I still recommend buying a pint to try out a color before covering the walls. And, one more suggestion: I use semi-gloss latex for almost everything. When painting raw wood, such as ready-to-finish furniture, a primer of Bin or Kilz is recommended. They also come in spray cans for small jobs, but are too expensive for using on a large piece of furniture.

ℬ Wall Cover-ups

If your walls are in need of repair, or if they are covered with old wallpaper or ugly paneling, the solution for transforming them might be to give them a faux finish. There are many decorative painting techniques that are perfect for camouflage and that create a look of rich elegance rather effortlessly and inexpensively. To create a faux finish you start with a base coat of paint over which you apply a translucent glaze. Then you create texture with techniques such as ragging, sponging, combing, or stippling. All of these techniques are easy to do by following the basic directions on the cans of materials or in the free booklets that are offered wherever the materials are sold, usually home centers.

Decorative Finishes

Several paint and stain companies have introduced their own line of faux finishes for the amateur crafter. None of these products requires lessons, prior knowledge, or any particular talent in the art department. For example, The Minwax Company, long known for their wood stains and refinishing products, makes a line of faux finishes called "Home Decor." They've taken all the guesswork out of the process by offering pint- and quart-size cans of premixed decorator paint colors. The line also includes glazes and all the tools, such as natural sponge and combs, for sponging and graining. All the paints and glazes are water based so they can be cleaned up easily and if you make a mistake it's easy to wipe it off and start over.

Sponging Is Easy

If you're sponging a wall, for example, you choose the base paint color and apply it to the entire area. When it dries, in about two hours, you mix equal parts of the same paint or a contrasting color with the glaze and apply it over the base paint. Then you use this to sponge over the surface. (See page 44) The directions on the cans are quite clear and they come with little booklets to give you the visuals.

All in One System

Lowe's home centers have their line called "Decorative Effects," manufactured by Valspar. It's basically the same system as that from Minwax except the glazes come in a variety of premixed colors to go over their base paints. All are water cleanup. The paints come in large cans and the glazes in easy-to-pour plastic bottles. The suggested use is for walls and floors, although I've used it successfully on furniture and small items as well. I especially like their base-coat paint colors, which range from the palest celadon green to steel gray. They offer unusual shades of decorator colors that you don't often find ready-mixed. These products come with how-to booklets for each technique and show photographs of finished rooms for inspiration.

Textured Wall

The following technique is not typically found in the how-to booklets. However, it's an easy way to create a subtle overall texture. You'll need: semigloss latex wall paint, paintbrush, water-based glaze, coffee can or dish for mixing, mixing stick, rubber gloves, plastic wrap (such as Saran or Handy Wrap).

Directions:

1. Begin by painting the walls with semigloss latex. Let dry.
2. Next, mix together equal amounts of paint and glaze and apply it to a section of the wall.
3. While the wall is wet, pull off a strip of plastic wrap and place it over the glazed area, allowing it to crinkle.
4. Pat it down and then carefully peel it away to reveal a textured pattern.
5. Continue to do this across the walls. Let dry overnight.

Other Materials for Different Effects

Using the same method as above, substitute a rolled-up rag, and starting from the center, roll the rag down the wall to the left, then the right, and so on. As the rag picks up the glaze, it will create an irregular and shaded texture of dark and light.

Distressed Wall

In my shop on Nantucket Island, one wall is faux distressed. I had intended to do all the walls this way, but after one I realized it was a lot of work and so I simply painted the others. I tell you this so you'll be forewarned. This is not an easy or quick process, but the results continue to get rave reviews and everyone wants to know how it was done. If you are willing to put in the time, you can create an interesting effect that would cost hundreds of dollars if you hired a professional to do it. The process is one of trial and error, but very forgiving because you can adjust the technique as you go along. The trick is to approach this project with complete confidence. Don't hesitate when applying the paint, tissue, or varnish. Just slap it on every which way and it will be a lot of fun.

1. Paint the entire wall with latex paint. I used an off-white color. Let dry.

2. Working on one section at a time and using a throw-away-type sponge brush, apply water-base, semigloss varnish to the wall.

3. The next step is messy and requires wearing rubber gloves. Crinkle large sheets of tissue paper and apply to the wet paint. Continue to apply sheets of tissue paper in this way, overlapping and moving it so there are folds and creases. Keep the tissue wet by applying the varnish over it as you work. Keep applying varnish and tissue in this way as you work across the wall. You can rip pieces of tissue and apply smaller and larger, even and irregular pieces of tissue to simulate a bumpy, uneven, distressed wall.

4. When completely covered, let the varnish dry overnight.

5. You can leave it as is or continue to add shading and color here and there. For this I used different-colored acrylic paints, which come in small tubes. I chose light blue, yellow, and gray and dabbed the paint color here and there in all the creases. Then I used a wet sponge brush to soften and rub the paint onto the background in irregular smudges. As you can see, this is a very loose and free-form style of faux finishing. Stand back and look at the overall effect while you're working. Then apply color wherever you think it's needed. There is no absolute way to do this. The creativity is up to the creator.

6. Let the acrylic paint dry for about two hours. Then apply a coat of the varnish over the entire wall. If you want to add more shading, use a raw or burnt umber acrylic and an artist's brush to dab the color here and there. Then use a dry, clean rag or piece of cheesecloth (available in home centers) to blend it in so it is subtle. The colors you add should never be obvious. The yellow will look like spots of dappled sunlight, the blue will add shadow, and the umbers will give the wall a look of aging.

ᏚᎧ Wood Paneling

You can cover unsightly walls or transform an uninteresting room with various kinds of easy-to-install wood paneling. The Georgia-Pacific Company makes quite a few different styles of solid wood plank paneling in a variety of widths and groove patterns. They also have plank paneling wainscot kits in knotty cedar or pine. Each kit contains plank paneling plus base and chair rail molding to cover fifteen and a half square feet of wall space. The planks are precut to wainscot height and the molding is rabbeted for a great fit. This might be an interesting idea for a dining room or any room in a summer cottage.

Bead Board

Beaded panels painted white look great; anyone interested can see what it looks like in my book *Nantucket Style*. It's featured in the house on Hither Creek. Georgia-Pacific also makes a prefinished, real wood, beaded groove panel called "Bedford Village" and it comes in bone white unfinished oak and a lot of other wood tones as well. The panels are 4 by 8 feet and $5/32$ inch thick.

Make a Small Room Seem Larger

Light-colored paneling appears to enlarge small areas and I've seen Millplank in rustic silver (Georgia-Pacific) applied on the diagonal for a really interesting look. It's a bit more rustic than the beaded board and comes in 4- by 8-inch panels that are 5/16 inch thick. All the paneling can be applied to studs sixteen inches on center or over a solid backer. They can be glued and nailed or simply nailed. These products are available from most large lumber companies.

ℬ Decorating with Paintings

Choosing artwork is tricky. It usually comes after a room or house is furnished. But I know many couples who buy art along with the rest of the furnishings as they go along. This makes sense. My friend Arthur who works in a gallery has a favorite shirt with the following saying, "Great art doesn't have to match the sofa." Ah, but a more important issue, does the sofa have to match the art?

Wall Colors to Display Art

Many readers ask if there's a good color for painting walls, one that will enhance their artwork. White is always safe, but many decorators use dark colors like charcoal gray and hunter green. Right now there is a trend moving toward colors and away from beiges. Hunter green has become a decorator's neutral as it dramatically offsets other colors, patterns, or designs.

Buying a Painting Can Lead to Trouble

Last year I fell madly in love . . . with an artist's work. The artist's collages were being featured at a local gallery and were created with shades of white and pastel papers among other bits and pieces of interest. I've coveted her work ever since I first saw it. However, not until the collages were in my house did I fully appreciate the joy of living with and looking at them daily. When one acquires a piece of artwork it's similar to bringing home a new baby. Something special has been added to your household, but it also affects and changes the dynamics of your environment. It impacts the rest of the furnishings in the room as a baby impacts the other members of your family. So bringing these four related pieces into my home has presented interesting challenges, beginning with the monumental decision of where to hang them.

Art Goes Everywhere

A woman came into my shop the other day and asked if it seemed in poor taste to hang artwork in the bathroom. "That's my favorite art gallery," I told her. "I display all my friends' artwork as well as framed photographs in our powder room. Guests usually enjoy the display." She explained that she couldn't afford paintings and has collected a variety of posters, photographs, and framed cards from her vacations. She felt that "real" art should be hung in the living room, while these "souvenir" hangings belonged in less prominent spaces. I assured her that many people hang photographs and other framed collectibles in all the rooms in their homes and it isn't a matter of cost but of what you enjoy looking at. Over the years my husband and I have purchased photographs by a handful of photographers whose work we especially like, and they hang where they look best.

How the Artists Do It

My artist friends approach decorating their spaces in a variety of ways. One has an interesting and eclectic collection of art throughout his house. But the most exciting arrangement is one that fills an entire wall of the den. The variety of work is vast and the array of framing is equally interesting.

Another artist friend mixes collages, paintings, assemblages, photographs, and collections. Every room, from the tiny entry hall to the kitchen to the dining room and the large living room, is a visual treat.

Still another displays a collection of paintings of a similar subject matter on the front stairway wall that's visible from the center hallway. It provides a dramatic display.

A quilter I know furnished her house in a modern style. She has an exciting red and white quilt filling an entire wall. The pattern is bold and graphic and while it's a country quilt the design is extremely contemporary-looking and adds warmth to the environment. (More about quilts on page 63).

Art Brings Pleasure

Whatever you hang on your walls, wherever you hang it, what matters most isn't the subject, the color, or whether it matches the sofa. The important thing is that it be a pleasure for you to look at it.

ஐ Decorating with Photographs

I always enjoy seeing family photographs displayed in pretty frames and this is a relatively inexpensive accessory. A grouping of different-size frames on an occasional table or on a mantelpiece over the fireplace always personalizes a home. My daughters take lots of pictures of their children and display them in interesting ways. Using these framed photographs as decorating accessories expresses where they are in their lives at this time.

Creating a Theme

My daughter Robby always gives photographs as gifts and offers some terrific ideas for creating an interesting collection. One of her favorite projects is to put together a collage of photos taken on a family vacation. She buys a frame that holds six photos. In this way she has a complete story in one frame that represents that particular family event. This might be any special occasion such as a birthday or Christmas get-together. The idea of displaying several photos in one frame is a nice twist on a familiar theme.

Photo Gift Ideas

Another photo idea came from my daughter Amy. For Christmas she had a calendar made with each month represented by a different-color Xerox copy of her family. As each month passes she tears off the photocopy and frames it. You can get this done at many office supply shops. But more than that, you can have all sorts of creative and personalized gifts made from photographs that go beyond the ordinary. Here are a few suggestions:

1. Put together a collage of personal items, such as dad's watch, dad's lucky coin, maybe a favorite photograph. The items can even be three-dimensional. Bring them to a copy center with scanning capabilities and they can make a print suitable for framing. You can personalize a picture with all sorts of meaningful items from a day at the beach, a picnic, a trip, or a special event. For example, take a piece of lace, a flower, a feather, any collectible, and have a photo made of your arrangement. Add a saying, sentiment, or names and give it to someone on his or her special day.

2. If you want to be truly manipulative, it's not a bad thing. That is, if it's photo manipulation. Maybe you have an old photograph of your grandfather. You can have a new photo made of you and your grandfather together from two separate photos. Or, if you have a group photo with a family member or friend in it, they can pick out that one person and enlarge only his or her image. You can be creative with old photographs, as well, by doctoring them to be different.

3. Have someone's picture superimposed onto the front of a favorite magazine. For example, put him on *Time* or a sports magazine with your own caption underneath.

4. Got a picture of your favorite weekend fisherman holding his tiny catch of the day? The fish can actually be enlarged in the photo (with the fisherperson next to it) so it's the size of the fish that got away—in fact, bigger!

5. Is your significant other bald or slightly overweight? It's a cinch to give him hair, slim him down, even turn a frown into a smile. Add some muscles while you're at it. Got a photo where the whole family looks great, except for dad? That can be altered so that dad is the best-looking guy in the bunch. And won't he be surprised!

6. If someone you know is an amateur athlete, cut out a ban-

ner headline from a world-famous person and use it to go with his or her photo.

7. An aspiring bestselling author? Turn him into the person of his dreams in an instant with your own version of *The New York Times* bestseller list, altered with his own book title and his name as author.

8. You can even make someone president of the United States! Just change the Commander-in-Chief's face.

9. An enlargement of any photograph is an inexpensive gift. In fact, have a poster made of the number one man in your life.

10. Look for interesting frames for any size photo you've cre-
ated. And finally, if a photo of your family isn't exactly what you had in mind, consider framing a photograph that you purchase at a local camera shop. There are hundreds to choose from and they are extremely affordable. Pick a photograph of something that has special meaning to your family.

ℰℑ Quilts As Art

Quilts and wall hangings, old and new, offer good value and good design as decorative accessories in any room. Quilts on beds, quilts as wall hangings, and quilts as table covers all add warmth and character even if your style isn't American country. In fact many two-color, geometric quilt patterns are quite contemporary looking. A bold graphic design similar to those of the Amish is compelling in any setting. I have seen large, wall-sized quilts dis-played in extremely modern office buildings as well as in a log cabin home, with equally dramatic impact. A beautifully designed wall hanging is a sensational substitute for more expensive art-work.

Timeless Designs

Early American quilt patterns are surprisingly timeless in design. This is perhaps why the original quilt patterns that were really quite naively conceived are still being reproduced, copied, and improvised over and over again to this day. Think about it—bear claws from footprints made in the snow, a log cabin, tumbling blocks, rose of Sharon, flying geese, fence rail—these were the images early quilters saw from their windows. They weren't designers, but they were looking for inspiration for designs they could interpret with cut pieces of fabric. Almost all the shapes are geometric and so didn't require an artist. It was really quite ingenious to develop so many different designs that are today considered classic.

Making Your Own

Depending on the fabrics and colors, there are endless possibilities for the creative quilter. I have written many quilting books and designed many quilts. One thing is obvious: If you can sew a straight line on a sewing machine you can make a quilt. So the technical part is easy. You just follow a pattern and simple directions. But choosing a pattern and the fabric prints and colors is what determines the look of it. For example, a combination of colorful calicos and gingham or homespun will surely result in a country quilt no matter what the design. But the same pattern can look quite different if rendered in two solid, contrasting colors like blue and white.

Start with a Wall Hanging

How do you start? I'd suggest a forty-two-inch-square wall hanging. Most traditional quilt patterns will work within the forty-two-inch square and it's practical because fabric comes forty-five inches wide so you won't have to piece the backing. It's manageable because it's small enough to fit on your lap for quilting, and because of its size, there's a good chance you'll finish it. (Many overly ambitious craft projects lie abandoned in scrap baskets.) Furthermore, it's a size that can fit on most wall spaces.

Quilt Patterns

Next, you'll want to find a pattern that appeals to you. Keep in mind that designs made from squares and triangles are the easiest to piece. I especially like to design projects with colors and prints, finding different ways to put them together so they look fresh. I also like hand-quilting better than piecing so I design projects that look best when hand-quilted. Many quilt makers like the machine work best, and so choose projects where hand-quilting isn't essential.

Log Cabin Is a Traditional Pattern

A log cabin pattern is made up of graduated sizes of rectangular strips of fabric built around a center square (the chimney). It is one of the few quilt patterns that looks good even if it isn't quilted. Try to imagine a log cabin quilt made from red, white, and lots of calico prints. The overall pattern is quite busy and very cozy looking. Now visualize the same pattern made from beige, eggshell, cream, buff, linen, winter white. Each fabric might have a different texture with one nubby, another percale, a damask, perhaps a muslin. Suddenly the country log cabin quilt becomes cool and contemporary. The same traditional pattern looks entirely different. There are literally hundreds of other ways to combine fabric to create a look for your taste using the same traditional pattern.

How to Do It

After you've chosen a pattern you like, get some grid paper and colored pencils. Draw the outline of the quilt and the pattern on it. Make copies of this so you can play around with different color combinations that work for you. Once you've designed your quilt you can buy the fabrics to create it. But be forewarned! Fabric shops can be downright addictive. I always get carried away and now have overflowing baskets of fabric for well-intentioned projects I plan to do someday. A trip to a fabric shop on a rainy day will give you an instant lift. It's like visiting a spring garden in full bloom.

Design Options

Another way to design your quilt is with scraps of cut-up fabric. Cut them to the size of the pieces on your paper pattern and glue them in place. You'll get a miniature view of what the full quilt will look like. You might also check with your local fabric shop or community activities listing to find out about quilting classes.

Baby Quilts

While I've made lots of quilts over the years, the one I am drawn to most is the baby quilt. Crib- and carriage-size quilts are fun to design and can be made rather quickly. Best of all a small quilt is the perfect wall hanging for a baby's room.

Crib Quilts As Collectibles

With the ongoing surge in collecting American folk art, collectors have become fascinated with crib quilts. In fact, fine crib quilts and Amish quilts (both of which were taken for granted for years but are now somewhat scarce) are two of the most sought-after items in the antiques market. Because crib quilts are small, they can be hung as textile paintings in spaces that cannot accommodate full-size quilts. Even at the dramatically increased prices recently recorded, they are still a bargain as original works of art.

A Bit of History

It's impossible to say who made the first crib quilt, but as with all quilts, these too were an invention born out of necessity, and they were made from scraps of worn clothing. The idea of quilting ties us to history, to the time when it was discovered that two layers of material filled with some light stuffing provided excellent protection and insulation against both heat and cold.

Easy to Make

I like to make a baby quilt from one yard of forty-five-inch-wide fabric and then add a two- to four-inch border of a corresponding print and color all around. This makes a practical size quilt that can be used in the crib or as a quilted wall hanging in the baby's room.

When used as a wall hanging, the border fabric acts as a frame for the printed design and can be hung either horizontally or vertically on the wall.

If you are interested in learning to make a quilt, a baby quilt is an excellent way to begin. Almost any patchwork pattern for a full-size quilt can be adapted for a crib-size quilt with the use of light colors and small fabric prints. The beginning of the fun in making a crib quilt is in selecting the fabrics.

Decorating with Antique Quilts

If you're more interested in purchasing an old quilt than making a new one, you can find many dealers in American folk art who sell them. If a quilt is quite old it can be framed and will make a lovely addition to any home. Early quilts made of geometric patchwork patterns can look surprisingly contemporary and fit in with any decorating scheme. In fact, they lend character as well as homespun warmth wherever they are displayed.

Quilts to Use

It is easy to find a wide selection of new and affordable baby quilts in patchwork, appliqué, and printed designs for everyday use. Some have an old-fashioned quality, especially when early patterns are copied. But the newer, brighter, and bolder designs seem more appropriate for today's lifestyle. Many baby quilts are made of a cotton blend for practical purposes, and they're designed for visual stimulation. Just as quilt makers responded to their environment a century ago, we too are responding to our modern environment.

ఌ Plates As Art

Many people collect plates and use them as a decorative element in their homes. The custom of hanging ceramics originated in Europe. Plates of all sorts were used to decorate walls, around mirrors, along a mantelpiece, and around the top of a wall below the crown molding. At least as far back as the Renaissance there were ceramic plates with holes in the backs for hanging. They were found in very ornate, formal homes as well as in simple country ones.

Today decorators often hang plates as they would a grouping of paintings. However, unlike framed art, hanging plates create dimension. They can provide pattern on a wall where none exists. And, unlike wallpaper, plates are easy to remove when you want a change.

When interior decorator Mario Buatta decorated the White House guest house he hung some of the old family china on the dining room walls. If you don't have old family treasures you can find pretty and inexpensive plates to use for decorating and no one will be the wiser.

Plates with Something in Common

Those who collect plates for decorative purposes often have specific themes, colors, or patterns they prefer. Some people only collect plates from a specific period, while others collect pretty plates, old and new, and mix them together. Creamware in different patterns, for example, makes a lovely display if you want a monochromatic traditional look. Antique Spode dishes with blue and white scenes are among some prized collectibles often displayed on a wall. There are also very lovely reproductions. Wedgwood is another collectible used this way. In fact, blue and white patterns seem to be the most popular theme, and they add interest in a room filled with blue and white fabrics.

Where to Find Interesting Plates

Many antique shops carry old and often valuable plates. Many better craft shops feature plates in all sorts of patterns, sizes, and shapes created by artisans. In gift shops we find fanciful, sophisticated, and whimsical plates such as those designed by Mackenzie-Childs. Early majolica and Quimper, both old and new, are among the popular collectible plates.

Hanging Plates

It's quite easy to hang plates. They look best when the holder isn't too conspicuous. Simple wrought-iron plate holders can be found in gift shops. They are made to display three, four, or five plates in a vertical row. In this way they can be a decorative element in a room, and also easily accessible for use. To display the plates on the wall you can also find simple, inexpensive spring-tension wire holders at most hardware stores. You can also find a variety of fancier holders such as brass ones with decorative elements on them, which hold one plate each. Also available are freestanding brass and wooden plate holders in different sizes for displaying one beautiful plate on a shelf or table.

Finding Plates in Unexpected Places

Finding a plate while traveling can become the basis for a collection. For one thing, a plate is easy to pack between clothing in a suitcase. Last year I brought back an entire set of classic blue-and-yellow-rimmed plates I found while traveling in Europe. The plates were easy to pack as we had brought bubble packing for this purpose.

Suggestions for a Collection

Mixing and matching plates for display and for use can provide one with an interesting hobby, a safe obsession, a focal point of interest when shopping, and even a valuable collection. If you want to start collecting plates here are a few suggestions: Limoges, Lusterware, Mochaware, Delft, Biscuit, Porcelain, Quimper, Faience, Spongeware, Staffordshire, Stoneware, Transferware, Wedgwood, Yellowware, and Spatterware.

Gathering Information

There are many good books devoted exclusively to collecting ceramics. Most are well-illustrated with everything from the history of pottery and porcelain in general, to those devoted to a specific type in detail. It's fascinating to read about different chinaware and in so doing you'll stumble on something that is particularly appealing to you. Sometimes a collection is created to add to the interior decor, but it can happen the other way around. You may find a collectible you love, and build your furnishings around the colors and patterns of the plates. Either way, these items will provide a nice focal point in a room.

Windows

ᏭᎧ Windows and Light

Windows can pose a decorating problem. By day we want them unobstructed so as to get as much light as possible into a room. But by night all those black panes aren't very attractive. "Light is an important decorating element," says New York decorator Michael Foster. "I like to use as much natural light as possible in my work." When planning the lighting in a room, it's good to understand the different possibilities and how to achieve them, naturally or artificially. The location of a window should be considered when deciding what sort of curtain, shade, or other treatment might look best.

Different Types of Light

The quality of light in an interior can vary greatly depending on the source and how it is treated. Most synthetic light is incandescent, which is primarily warm, and it makes objects look yellow. Fluorescent light is usually cool light, making color appear more blue or violet. Artifical lighting that comes close to imitating natural sunlight is now available.

Balanced Light

Natural sunlight is often referred to as balanced, full-spectrum light. What this means is that it contains all the "spectral colors," or colors of the rainbow, which merge into clear, colorless light. Full-spectrum light is balanced, and the colors of furnishings will look their truest under it. Even natural light, however, tends to become unbalanced when one part of the spectrum that tends toward cool, or warm-colored light, predominates. This can happen with atmospheric conditions or when light enters from only one direction, as in most natural light sources in most homes.

North Light

Perhaps you've heard that artists prefer studios with a north light. This is because light entering through the north is the clearest, and it provides even and consistent light. Often considered "cold light," it has a cool, bluish cast and in northern climates builders limit the number of windows on the northern side because it is the coldest exposure. For energy conservation these windows are often treated with insulated shades. Hunter Douglas's Duette honeycomb shades are good for this because they trap the air in the honeycomb cells. Lined draperies and cornices are also good here.

Eastern Light

Eastern or morning light is warmer and brighter, but also clear because impurities from the previous day have had a chance to settle during the night. Eastern light is also the most balanced, or full-spectrum, light. However, its brightness and clarity may render it warm, especially in the morning. East-facing rooms tend to heat up quickly and may hold the heat during the day. These windows are often treated with materials that diffuse the light, especially in summer. A good covering might be a light-control blind or pleated shade. To block out early light in bedrooms, take advantage of the room-darkening options available in pleated shades.

Windows Facing West

Light from west-facing windows is the warmest in color and the hottest physically since the atmosphere heats up during the day. It is also often hazy, as the impurities of the day linger until nightfall. Because prolonged exposure to this strong light can be damaging to wood furniture and colored fabrics, especially in summer, windows should generally be covered with a combination of light-diffusing, UV-ray-protecting treatments. Horizontal louvers or wood blinds and shutters work well here since the light can be admitted but diffused onto the ceiling or floor. Hunter Douglas has a new SoftSuede matte-textured finish blind that adds a soft, glare-free look at the window. Vertical blinds offer superior light control for window walls and large window expanses. I think they look a little too institutional, but that's just a personal thing.

Southern Exposure

South-facing windows are the most important natural light source because they receive sunlight year-round and cast a warm, golden glow on interiors. However, this light will cause the greatest damage to your furnishings. Roller shades in opaque fabrics, Vignette window shadings, an updated Roman shade with gently contoured fabric folds that roll up into a sleek headrail, and Duette shades with triple layers of honeycombs are all good choices for a southern exposure.

Location Is Everything

Here's another consideration. The manner in which light falls into a room is also affected by window location. Windows high on an exterior wall admit light deep into the room, while low or wide windows bring in the light in shallow baths. Several windows in small rooms will offer a more even distribution of natural light as will a group of windows in a large space.

Light Where You Want It

I like the Duette shade with the top-down/bottom-up hardware. It allows the shade to stack at the bottom to let in light from above, but still provides privacy. Study each room in your house in regard to location of windows and the type of light they afford. In this way you'll treat them in a manner that will allow you the right light for maximum beauty and comfort in your home.

ℬ Window Treatments

New and improved window treatments are available and constantly updated. If you want to cover your windows in style with the least amount of effort, there are quite a few ways to do this. If you can find one treatment that works for all your windows, it will not only save you money (buying many can often result in a deep discount) but the continuity from room to room will look best.

Innovative Window Coverings

Springs Window Fashions offers a clever innovation to make life easier and more convenient: remote-controlled, motorized window shades and blinds. This has to be the ultimate for confirmed couch potatoes and I for one want to be a member of this club. The battery-operated Auto Vue automated blind system is so inexpensive that many more people will now have one less reason to get up and walk across the room. In fact, to make things even easier, they have a remote control unit so you can open all your window coverings from a single remote! If this remote blind system appeals to you, you might like to know that it operates with a motor and microchip that fits invisibly inside a standard headrail and that it will operate for up to three years on four AA-size batteries. In other words, no electrician is needed for installation.

This window treatment is a great advantage for tall windows or out-of-the-way windows where it's inconvenient or dangerous to operate blinds or shades manually. Aside from the remote control feature, these blinds also offer a light sensor option that opens and closes window coverings automatically in response to changing light conditions. This is a terrific feature for homeowners who don't occupy their homes on a full-time basis. Your home is more secure because it has a lived-in look, even when you're not there to open and close the blinds. Auto Vue is available on most models of Graber or Nanik blinds, pleated shades, and vertical blinds, and you can find them through retailers nationwide if you look under these names in the Yellow Pages under "blinds" or "window shades."

ぞう Window Blinds

Remember when miniblinds were all the rage? Now they seem passé. They were the modern version of our parents' or grandparents' classic 1930s Venetian blinds. Well, wooden blinds are now back in vogue and they are very similar to those old blinds of a few generations back, but they are sleeker and much better-looking. Surprisingly, they look modern. As with clothing styles, well-designed items for home decorating always come back in style.

A Custom Look

If you've been searching for a custom window treatment look you'll be happy to know you can now get it through the mail. Smith + Noble, a mail-order source in California, offers a catalog for ordering custom window treatments like wooden blinds in various sizes, colors, and finishes as well as shutters and blinds. The company provides swatches of fabrics and materials used in their window treatments so you can see and feel the product before making a purchase. One example of their custom products is Natural Roman Shades in hard-to-find materials like woven reeds, grasses, and woods.

What Is a Blind?

A blind is a window covering made of either horizontal or vertical slats that can be rotated for light and privacy control. Horizontal blinds may be drawn up and vertical blinds may be drawn to the side for an unobstructed view.

What Is a Shade?

A shade is a window covering made of a piece of material that rolls, gathers, or folds both up and down. The shade can be raised for light and view and lowered for privacy.

What Is a Shutter?

A shutter has a hinged frame, filled with louvers or panels, that attaches directly to the window frame. While the louvers are often opened for air and light, the frames usually remain closed.

Defining Curtains

Curtains are an expanse of fabric gathered on a rod. Curtains are opened and closed by simply pushing the fabric from side to side.

Defining Draperies

A drapery is an expanse of pleated fabric suspended from a number of metal hooks. The hooks are generally attached to a mechanical rod that allows the fabric to be closed, drawn open, or gathered to the side.

Wood Blinds

The newest in wood blinds are made of basswood and are not affected by extreme temperatures and humidity. They come with one-, two-, or three-inch slats, and the cloth tapes that adjust and hold the individual blinds and run down both sides of the front of the blinds can be ordered in dozens of styles and colors, including a safari print, as well as linen in different colors to match your wall paint. The wood slats have a smooth, satiny finish or you can get a more rustic look with the interesting grain finished in a low sheen. For a rugged look there are sandblasted slats that show the natural grain through the paint.

Decorative Tapes

While you can get blinds with color-coordinated nylon ladders so unobtrusive that they nearly disappear, the decorative tapes are quite interesting. There is a European-looking two-tone herring-bone design that adds texture and comes in seven colors, as well as woven, textured designs like damask.

New and Improved Shutters

Shutters have changed considerably from the days when I painted unfinished, rather flimsy shutters ordered from the Sears catalog. Sturdy basswood shutters are precut and predrilled and crafted for easy installation. You can choose your color and finish, the number of panels, even the color of the hardware. Delivery of most items is a week if you pay for delivery, or two weeks for free delivery.

Custom Treatments

If you want custom-made curtains, shades, and balloon or Roman shades, for example, you can order these in a variety of sub-tle colors and pretty fabrics such as damask, silks, velvets, linens, burlap, chenille, and canvas just to name a few.

Smith + Noble catalogs give measuring and ordering informa-tion as well as a price list: *Windoware Sourcebook* is an informative and inspirational guide to window treatments, and *Windoware* gives decorating ideas, advice, and tips to help homeowners dress their windows fashionably while limiting the amount of time and money spent. You can obtain them for free by calling: 1 (800) 765-7776.

Art Under Foot

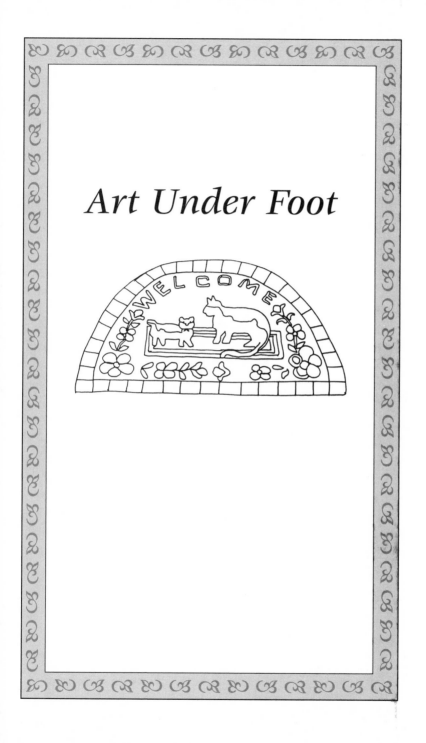

Wood Floors and Furniture Care

Good maintenance is the easiest and cheapest way to keep your home looking its best. Did you know that the same winter air that dries out our skin plays havoc with solid hardwood floors and furniture? Because they're natural materials, hardwoods respond to changes in the humidity around them. Hardwood floors and furniture are built to expand and contract safely as the air's moisture content rises and falls with the seasons. Still, when the weather is cold outside, you'll want to take a little extra care to protect your hardwoods from superdry air inside your home.

Humidity

Once your furnace starts running, the Hardwood Manufacturers Association recommends using a humidifier to keep your home's relative humidity around 30 percent. How does one measure 30 percent? Their suggestion: "If you feel comfortable yourself, without that dry, scratchy, winter-air feeling, you'll be pretty close."

If the relative humidity is much lower than that, tabletop sections may contract and separate a bit. Spaces between floorboards may be exaggerated. Fortunately, these dry-air changes correct themselves when humidity rises, and the gaps disappear harmlessly. So, if you see separations between boards or joints, it's reassuring to know they aren't permanent.

Hardwood Is Hardy

Even after a century of adapting to weather cycles, hardwood products keep the strength and good looks they had when they were new. During the winter your skin needs a little extra attention and so will the hardwoods in your home. Here are a few tips:

1. Store tabletop leaves near the table itself. Never store them in a damp basement.
2. Avoid placing solid hardwood furniture directly in front of radiators or other heat sources.
3. Don't expose finely finished surfaces to constant direct sunlight.
4. Make sure boots and shoes are free of snow, salt, and outdoor debris before walking on hardwood floors. Use mats inside and outside all entrances to your home.
5. Solid hardwood furniture looks best if it's dusted weekly with a soft cloth, and waxed or polished every six to twelve months. Follow the grain of the wood.

Better Furniture

Solid hardwood furniture is growing in popularity. Many young people are discovering better furniture lines such as those from Heywood-Wakefield or Herman Miller. They are really noticing construction quality, and they want solid furniture that's built to last. Manufacturers are responding to the changes in consumer tastes with new lines of furniture. This represents a significant departure for a high-end industry that has been dominated by veneer construction for many years. This difference in construction methods gives solid hardwood furniture a distinct edge in durability.

Heywood-Wakefield, founded in 1826, is enjoying renewed interest in its solid hardwood furniture of ash, maple, and birch. While the company's original pieces are commanding top dollar in antique furniture shops, newer, less expensive Heywood-Wakefield products also are gaining recognition.

Furniture As an Investment in the Future

Aminy L. Audi, vice president of L. & J. G. Stickley, the venerable solid hardwood furniture maker in New York City says, "There is no question that if a family with young children wants to enjoy their furniture, purchasing solid wood is a very solid investment for the future." He goes on, "You can strip, sand, and refinish a solid wood piece several times during its lifetime. You don't have that option with veneer."

The Arts and Crafts Movement

In 1989 Stickley began reproducing many of the oak Arts and Crafts and Mission-style pieces that the Stickley brothers first created in the early 1900s. In 1991 they added cherry in response to people's wishes to have the simple, clean lines of a wood that ages beautifully and presents an elegant-looking grain. It's good to know that if you want the classic good looks of styles from that period you don't have to go to an expensive antique store to find it. The reproductions offer good, lasting value.

Veneer Versus Hardwood

The differences between veneer and solid hardwood construction are significant, but not always obvious. Veneers are thin slices of wood that are often bonded to a reconstituted wood product, such as particleboard. By contrast, all visible parts of solid hardwood furniture are made of hardwood lumber. For this reason, manufacturers like Stickley are making an effort to educate consumers. As solid hardwood furniture appears more and more often in furniture stores, consumers are getting better at recognizing its construction. Don't be afraid to pull out drawers and turn over tables in an effort to become educated as to what to look for. As you learn more, you'll be inclined to check for details such as the dovetail joints that characterize solid hardwood drawers when shopping for furniture. In the end you'll make educated purchases.

More Information

For more information on selecting and caring for solid hardwood furniture you can visit the Hardwood Information Center on the World Wide Web: http://www.hardwood.org., or call for a free booklet: 1 (800) 373-WOOD.

℘ Creating Fabulous Floorcloths

Painted canvas floorcloths fit right in with our current interest in American folk art and country-style decorating. Floorcloths were quite popular in both European and American homes in the eighteenth and nineteenth centuries. In fact, the earliest floor coverings in American homes were painted canvas, often with geometric designs to look like tiles. They were used as an economical substitute for carpeting. Originally, most were painted freehand by artisans. Later, stenciling provided a quicker and easier way for the layperson to create a repeated and intricate design. The painted surface is then protected with several layers of polyurethane so it can be walked on and cleaned with mild soap and water.

How a Floorcloth Is Made

A floorcloth is made from heavy artist's canvas that has been primed with paint on one side and decorated with a painted illustration, a decorative painting technique, or a stencil design. Once the size is determined, you would add a few inches of material all around before cutting out the canvas. After the background is painted, the extra inches are turned to the back of the canvas and glued to create a heavy and finished edge all around.

Where to Use a Floorcloth

Originally, floorcloths provided a means for covering unattractive floors, and since they are light, they could be moved from room to room. Today they offer the same promise of adding an attractive accent in an entryway, in front of a fireplace hearth, in a kitchen, or on a larger scale, in covering an entire room.

An Inexpensive Do-It-Yourself Project

Since most floorcloths are painted by professional artisans, they can be quite expensive to purchase. However, the materials are inexpensive and readily available in art supply stores and there are many painting techniques easily learned by a novice. Floorcloths are made from pretreated artists' canvas that you buy on a roll and then cut to the desired size. Some art stores will sell you precut sizes.

The best way to start is with a manageable size, such as two feet by four feet, which is perfect for a mat you might place inside a doorway or in front of the kitchen sink. It's also a good size for a powder room. The background can be simply painted, or if you want a more interesting background, try a faux finish technique. Once you've created a textured background you can leave it as is or add a stencil design to the center or a border design around the edges.

Sponging Floorcloths Like a Pro

In our studio we often sponge-paint the background of our floorcloths with a subtle, but contrasting color. For example, if the background is lemon yellow, we might use a soft linen-white glaze for a cloudlike sponge painting.

1. Cut the mat two inches larger, all around, than the desired finished size. Paint the front of the canvas with your choice of latex paint color. Let dry.

2. Next apply a glaze. For best results use a glaze that is a shade darker or lighter than the base paint. For example, you might use a red base coat with a dark green glaze on top.

3. If the mat is small (two feet by four feet), coat the entire mat with the glaze mixture. If it's quite large, work in sections since the object is to apply a faux technique while the glaze is wet.

4. The glaze is translucent and will stay wet for quite a while so you can redo it if you mess up. The easiest technique is sponging, so this might be a good way to treat a first project. Using a damp, natural, sea sponge, pounce the sponge over the glaze to achieve a texture. Continue to do this until you have a subtle, blended background. You don't want big splotches. Go over and over the glaze with a soft rolling motion, changing the angle of your hand with each pounce. Add more of the glaze if needed.

How to Rag

Another easy technique is ragging. For this you will need paper toweling, a cheesecloth, or a terry washcloth. Try each on a painted board coated with glaze to see which texture you like best. Twist and roll up the material, and starting from one corner, roll the twisted rag diagonally across the glaze to the opposite corner. As you roll the rag it will pick up glaze and leave a texture behind revealing the paint color beneath the glaze.

Another interesting effect can be achieved with plastic food wrap rolled and twisted and applied in the same way. Or, you might wad up a cloth and use it to create texture by pressing it firmly to the glazed surface. Repeat this over and over for an interesting texture. If you don't like the effect the first time, it's easy to brush more glaze over it and start again. After sponging or ragging, let it dry overnight.

To Finish

1. To create a border, begin by measuring in two inches from the outside edges and draw an outline at this point. The extra two inches will be turned and glued to the back of the canvas to create a finished edge all around.

2. Before turning the edges, the corners should be mitered. To do this, draw a diagonal line from the outside corner edge to the inside drawn corner. Cut along this line. Fold the excess canvas back over itself and cut away these little triangles.

3. To keep your creases sharp, use a straightedge or metal ruler against the drawn lines and turn the two-inch canvas border to the back.

4. You can use a regular craft glue, such as Elmer's, to secure the canvas to the back, but I like to use a hot glue gun because it creates a stronger bond. If you use craft glue, be sure to weight it down with heavy books or something like that, overnight.

5. To finish and protect your painted floorcloth, apply a coat of clear polyurethane. Let dry and apply two or three more coats. When thoroughly dry, your floorcloth will be a sturdy and attractive addition to your room.

Stenciling a Floorcloth Design

Border patterns can be made up of repeat florals, leaves, or geometric designs. You'll find a variety of precut stencils in a well-stocked craft and hobby shop or in art supply stores. They come in different widths as well. A stencil is a sheet of thin plastic or waxed paper with the pattern cut away.  The stencil is taped in place on the floorcloth and paint is applied to the cutout area with a special stencil brush. When the stencil is removed the painted design remains on the background. I use acrylic paint for all stenciling projects.

Wallpaper Borders

There are many ways to decorate a floorcloth once it is painted. Wallpaper borders are easy to apply and provide a decorative finish much like a stencil. Once the background paint or faux finish has been applied and is thoroughly dry, measure and cut strips of wallpaper border for each side of the floorcloth.

Spread craft glue generously over the back of each strip and apply it to the front of the mat. Using a slightly damp sponge smooth the wallpaper down and wipe away any excess glue that seeps out from the edges. Use a rolling pin or wallpaper roller to further secure the wallpaper border to the floorcloth. Be sure all edges are glued down.

Create a Holiday Floorcloth

A floorcloth designed with a Christmas motif is a great way to add a bit of holiday cheer inside your front door. Sponge-paint the background with contrasting pale green paints, then stencil a border of repeat holly leaves and berries, or a tree pattern. When dry stencil the word "CHEERS" in the center of the floorcloth.

The Best Use for Your Floorcloth

A painted floorcloth should never be used on top of a rug because the rigid surface of a painted floorcloth will not give. It is not pliable and will not bend. The best way to use a painted floorcloth is on a hardwood or tile floor.

For summer use, consider placing a floorcloth on the deck. This is a great way to decorate your outdoor living space. Since the painted canvas is covered with several coats of polyurethane it is relatively waterproof.

ℰℴ Hooked Rugs

While not as popular as quilts, early hooked rugs have managed to hold their own and continue to increase in value. However, you can still find affordable old rugs in good condition, and even newer, less expensive rugs add a touch of old-fashioned charm to any room. Best of all you can find designs and colors to suit any decorating scheme.

Popular Designs

Perhaps more than any other factor, collectors of hooked rugs are charmed and intrigued by their naive and simplistic designs. Since even the oldest hooked rugs date only from the mid-1800s, knowledgeable dealers admit that a rug's age is often less significant than its design.

Dating and cataloging hooked rugs is a favorite pastime of collectors, art historians, and dealers. Hooked rugs are significant in documenting our country's history. Just as early quilt makers drew inspiration from daily life and the scenes they saw around them, so did the rug makers. Their subject matter was usually a neighborhood scene, an idyllic landscape of the imagination, a boat, or a house and garden. Some of the scenes were quite realistic, others more primitively drawn. Further inspirations for designs were found in wallpaper patterns, furniture decoration, and embroidery.

A Collectible with an Interesting Past

Many of the earliest hooked rugs that survive today come from maritime settlements. The long, inactive periods at sea led to the invention of all sorts of crafts such as scrimshaw, macramé, and an early, primitive form of rug hooking in which sailors used bits of raveled burlap to create maritime scenes on rough linen ground. Early sailors' rugs often pictured ships, a motto, and the name of the vessel.

Grenfell Rugs

You might enjoy looking for a rug with an interesting history. The Grenfell Mission was established in the 1890s by Dr. Wilfred Grenfell, a physician devoted to relieving poverty, sickness, and exploitation along the northern coast of Newfoundland. The poor natives were gifted artisans who made distinctive hooked rugs depicting scenes of northern life.

In order to conserve materials, these rug makers used worn underwear and silk stockings that they cut into very narrow strips. This resulted in the dense, even pile characteristic of Grenfell rugs. There was a popular saying at the time, "When your stockings run, let them run to Labrador." The Grenfell rugs were sold throughout the United States and did much to promote the craft of rug hooking. Popular subjects were puffins, dog teams, a lone polar bear, arctic hunters, and the colors were mostly somber shades of blues, grays, black, browns, and greens.

Homey, Extraordinary Rugs

Rugs that evoke personal images or memories, that impart a message, or are linked to family life are never ordinary. The messages found in these rugs range from the intensely personal to the profound or simple and straightforward. Some are quite humorous, while others have barbed or ironic messages hooked into them. Relatives by marriage, for example, were often the subject for humorous as well as spiteful sayings. Wives also vented emotions about their spouses in pictures and words, making these rugs among the earliest expressions of women's liberation.

Rugs That Say Something

Not all storytelling rugs carry an original legend. Some repeat a favorite line from a poem or song; others carry a phrase that describes the illustration. Many "saying" rugs contain misspelled words. The most common message rugs are the little "Welcome" mats placed by the door. These have always been worked in a half circle to fit the sill of the door with the words worked across the bottom edge. The individual designs are as varied as the makers, but the message is unmistakable. A rug such as this at your front or back door would be delightful.

By the Hearth

"Home Sweet Home" hearth rugs were found by the fireplace in every nineteenth-century home. The lettering was often copied from a cross-stitch sampler and bore a resemblance to those careful creations. These message rugs have been made since rug hooking began and have never gone out of vogue.

Pretty Rugs

Bouquets, garlands, and baskets of flowers sometimes combined with fruits were popular subjects for early rug makers. The majority of old patterns were floral designs. Many elaborately detailed florals were made by the French of Acadia and Nova Scotia, often patterned after French textiles. The design might be a realistic bouquet, or a center motif surrounded by delicate garlands of soft colors or scrolls worked in pale rose and violet with a background of deep ivory. In New England, a floral rug's background is more likely to be a brown or soft tan to match the pinewood floors.

Many well-designed florals were made in Waldoboro, Maine, and Durham, New Hampshire. Of greatest value are the florals with white backgrounds. Many of these early rugs are incredibly detailed and show excellent craftsmanship in the use of colors and shading. Again, a floral hooked rug needn't be old to lend beauty to your home. Remember, it's the look you're after and it's often difficult to distinguish an old rug from a new one.

Patchwork Patterns

If you're looking for an accessory for a bedroom in which you've covered the bed with a patchwork or appliqué quilt, you can find rugs to go with this theme. Rugs combining a pattern of squares with alternating patterns of flowers were a step beyond the simple geometric rugs. These rugs bear a striking resemblance to appliqué quilts in which floral blocks alternate with pieced blocks. Alternating squares of florals and geometrics gave the rug maker an opportunity to be creative with the placement and arrangement of patterns, use up leftover scraps, and make the rug any size.

Pets Immortalized

An endless procession of household pets has been immortalized by devoted owners, in hooked portraits. Early rug makers honored their favorite cats, dogs, cows, pigs, hens, and horses. In the nineteenth and early twentieth centuries, horses were central to daily life, both as transportation and farm labor,  and for recreational purposes. As a result they are the subject of countless early rugs. Birds were also common subjects. The American eagle figured prominently in patriotic rugs.

Learn to Do It Yourself

Many people are fascinated with the craft of rug hooking: taking classes, reading how-to books, and trying it on their own. It's an easy craft to learn and the materials are few. Historically, rug hooking has always responded to the prevailing economic and cultural climate. It has provided a means of income in lean times, a pleasant diversion during a depression, a leisure-time activity for periods of prosperity, and now a medium for contemporary craftworkers.

For those who would like to try making a rug, there are many books available offering detailed step-by-step instructions.

Room by Room

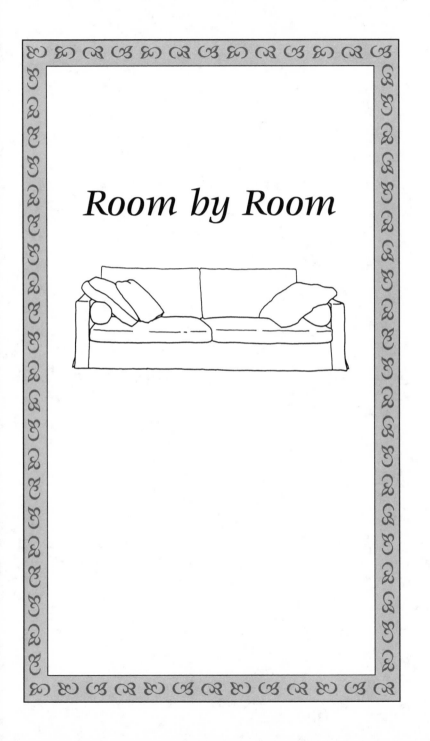

৪৩ Living Rooms

The only item you should spend real money on is a good sofa. Comfortable upholstered furniture isn't something you get at second-hand stores. However, if you aren't in a hurry to furnish your living room, you can always wait for a great sale on the items you need. Furthermore, it's good to know that if you stick with the floor models and don't start special ordering fabric for the sofa or chairs you choose, you will save a great deal.

Getting Around the Sofa Issue

My initial point notwithstanding, it's not necessary to own a sofa. There are many alternative ways to create a comfortable seating arrangement. I prefer two love seats and comfortable armchairs because I like to change the position of furniture from time to time and it's easier to do this with lighter furniture. A bench, pull-up side chairs, ottomans, and other small pieces of furniture can be used to create an interesting arrangement of furniture if you aren't ready for the sofa commitment.

Planning Storage Space

For those with smallish homes, rooms often have to serve several purposes. Sparse but carefully selected furnishings and lots of good storage are key in making it work. One wall devoted to a storage unit can accommodate all your electronic equipment with plenty of shelves for books and knickknacks as well as drawers for storing other items. Modular units are available in all price ranges. When looking at the unit, keep in mind that it will be filled with your "stuff." In this way you might feel you can get away with a piece of furniture that isn't made with the best wood, for example, one that might be less expensive but really won't be scrutinized for quality. As long as the item is sturdy and does the job you'll find it disappears once your things are arranged on the shelves.

Small Wooden Pieces

End tables, coffee tables, occasional tables, and chairs are pieces of furniture you *can* often find in secondhand stores, flea markets, yard sales, and auctions. If the lines are good and things are in good working order—in other words, drawers slide easily in and out—but the finish isn't perfect, you can always make it over. Paint is the easiest way to clean up a  good but "seen better days" piece of furniture, but throughout the book you'll learn how to do all sorts of faux finishing techniques to make something really special.

Carpets and Rugs

There are many floor coverings in every price range. When you decide what kind of carpet or rug is best for your room, educate yourself before making a final purchase. Several trips to a good floor covering shop will help you do this.

The Oriental Alternative

If you love Oriental rugs, for example, but can't afford the real thing, check out the reproductions. Once they're on your floors it really is hard to tell the real from the copy. I often buy rugs at auction for a fraction of what they would cost from a rug dealer.

The Natural Way

Sisal, a natural fiber, is another alternative to expensive floor covering. Decorators use this as a good solution when they want a practical, natural background. You can get sisal in colors as well. It is sold in room sizes or by the yard for wall-to-wall installation. Check out catalogs from Pottery Barn and Crate & Barrel for these items at the lowest possible prices.

Instant Window Solution

Plain white-paneled drapes are the best buys for a no-frills window treatment. However, if this seems boring, it's easy to customize them to go with your decorating scheme. Trim the edge with decorative braid or a strip of fabric to match the rest of the room. Make tie-backs from silk braid with tassel ends and you'll have a sensational look that doesn't cost a king's ransom.

Coffee Table Alternative

A friend of mine who travels a lot always brings her treasures home in wicker trunks purchased along the way. Once home she uses the trunks as end tables, a coffee table, at the end of a bed, wherever she needs a surface and storage. Have a piece of glass cut at a hardware store to fit the top of the trunk and you have an inexpensive table. Trunks are available at novelty stores and places like Pier 1 Imports. For added interest, spray-paint a natural-colored trunk in a bright color.

℘ Dining Rooms

Dining rooms are used for all sorts of family activities that have nothing to do with eating. Kids do homework on the dining room table. We play games on the dining room table and people often spend leisurely Sunday morning breakfasts with the newspaper spread out upon the dining room table. If you're fortunate to have a room set aside specifically for eating you probably know the joy of having any meal, be it breakfast or Thanksgiving dinner, in this room.

Making Dining Special

It doesn't cost much to make mealtime seem special. This is where many of us use things we may have inherited from family members: pretty tablecloths or placemats, ornate silverware, cut glass goblets, napkin rings, and candlesticks. None of these things seem out of place in the dining room. Of all the rooms in the house, the dining room is perhaps the least likely to be redecorated once it's done. It is in this room that you can express your talents with creative table settings, artistically arranged flowers, and culinary delights.

Decorating a Dining Area

Even if you don't have a separate room for dining and entertaining, you can create a wonderful oasis in a dining area that is either an extension of the living room or a space created as part of the kitchen. Room divider screens, for example, are perfect for closing off the kitchen area when you have guests. They take up very little room when folded and stored flat against the wall for everyday convenience. Another way to separate the cooking and eating areas is with visual tricks. You might hang a vertical row of pretty plates on a narrow wall between the areas. Hanging plants also serve as a visual divider. One friend has a large potted tree between the kitchen and eating areas.

Paint

There are a lot of interesting ways to paint the walls of a dining room or separate dining area. This is one time when you don't have to be conventional. In fact it can be fun to walk into a dining room and be surprised by the color. Paint has to be the cheapest way to create a new look and a specific mood. I've seen magnificent dining rooms in bright red, dark charcoal, pale coral, and celery green and each had a totally different feeling. If you mix your paint color with glaze it will give a rich finish to any painted wall.

Wallpaper

Wallpaper can give your dining room instant personality. The wall covering might be a busy and bright pattern such as a print of big cabbage roses or a more subdued overall print that might suggest a country style. There are literally thousands of wallpaper patterns and if you want to save money applying wallpaper yourself, it isn't a very difficult job. Always select prepasted papers if you're a beginner.

If you want to get the finished effect that wallpaper can provide, consider applying a wallpaper border or papering only half the wall, either top or bottom, with the wallpaper border finishing the dividing edge. Keep in mind that an overall repeat pattern is the easiest to work with. Stripes are the most difficult to match perfectly. Finally, if you like the look of a faux-finish treatment such as sponging or ragging, but don't feel confident doing this yourself, you can get wallpaper that simulates the different techniques. Once the paper is applied to your walls, you almost can't tell they aren't actually painted.

Wainscoting

This is the molding that is applied to the wall around the room just at chair height. Wainscoting is a decorative molding, but also serves a practical purpose, which is to keep chairs from marring the wall. Decorative molding is available at most home centers and lumberyards and it's easy to apply. You can either paint it to match the walls, or choose a color that is found in the wallpaper, or paint it in a contrasting color. When wallpaper is applied to the bottom portion of a wall, the wainscoting is then adhered to the wall over the top edge of the paper to give it a finished look.

Molding

There are many styles of wood molding that come in a variety of widths. Molding is often used to add an element of architectural interest to a room where none exists. This is an easy and inexpensive way to make a room grander, more elegant, or to create a specific style such as Federal or early American, depending on the molding. Some are carved with very elaborate designs, others are rounded or beveled or simply plain. You buy it in long strips and cut it to fit your walls. They can be stained, painted, or faux finished before applying to the walls.

The Dining Room Table

For years I used a beat-up old table for dining and always kept a tablecloth over it. If you find a secondhand table that needs refinishing but don't have the time, cover it until you can tackle this project. Even outdoor furniture can be concealed for indoor use if you don't have the money right away or haven't yet found the perfect table for your needs.

What Size Table Should You Buy?

The biggest problem most people have is determining the size of the table they need for the space. Remember, you need enough room to pull chairs away from the table and walk between the walls and backs of the chairs without asking anyone to pull forward. My suggestion is to buy the largest table you can fit into the space. If there are just one or two of you, get one with extra leaves for expansion when you have guests.

Shape Is Important

The shape of a table—rectangle, square, oval, or round—can determine the feeling of dining style. For example, a round table is the most intimate and encourages everyone to talk to one another rather than just to the person to their right or left. Most formal dining is associated with oval- or rectangular-shaped tables. A round table with an extension leaf will be turned into an oval—a good way to accommodate more than four.

Lighting

It's nice to be able to control the lighting in a dining room. If possible, put a dimmer switch on your lighting control. A chandelier over the table is nice, but always add candlelight. The more candles, the better. Votive candles can be placed at every place setting. When using tall candlesticks, make sure they do not interfere with easy communication from one end of the table to the other. A low table lamp gives off nice ambient light on a small table in the corner of the room or on a side table.

Other Pieces of Furniture

A china cupboard is a convenient place to store your dishes and glasses. If it has drawers or shelves behind doors, this is a good place to store table linens. While armoires and other large pieces of furniture can be expensive, these items can be found at ready-to-finish stores for a fraction of the price, and they're easy to stain, paint, or faux finish.

A sideboard is great for serving or for buffet dining. This table can be any size that will conveniently fit into the space. One couple I know who have recently bought a new home have a narrow wall area on one side of sliding glass doors that lead to a patio. Their solution is to hang a shelf along the wall and create a grouping of artwork around a mirror on the wall over the shelf. This will allow room for a larger table than would have been possible if they had had a standing piece of furniture in the room as well.

Finishing Touches

Collections and artwork add a personal touch to the room. Some people like to display plates, either hanging on the wall or on a shelf around the room. A large vase of flowers or flowering plants keeps the room looking fresh even when not in use. The dining room is an interesting place for bookshelves. A decorator friend had bookshelves built around the windows on one wall in her dining area. A small but comfortable chair and reading lamp in one corner of the room extend its use from time to time. If you have a nice view from a window, consider placing a mirror on the opposite wall to reflect that scene.

✂ Kitchens

A kitchen is the one area most of us want to keep functioning optimally at all times. If your kitchen is neat and organized, this is the beginning of achieving the look you want, whether it's a warm and homey country-style eat-in room or a modern, streamlined work space.

Getting Organized

Isolate and look critically at each area of the kitchen. Arrange the things you use most often in the most convenient places. If you're tight on space, use it wisely. For example, large trays, serving platters, and punch bowls used only during the holidays take up a lot of permanent space. Find an out-of-the-way place to keep them, perhaps in a china cabinet in another room or even in the basement. If you have duplicates, try to weed out. If there are things you use occasionally, try to fit them elsewhere. Even if your kitchen is quite large, you still want to organize things for optimum convenience.

A Little Goes a Long Way

Some of the "organizing gurus" whom I know keep two lists. One is the short, quick project list, the other is the one with more ambitious projects that may or may not get done. I like this approach because there's always something to do that can get you closer to the ultimate goal, and if you never get to the big projects, you're still ahead of the game. Don't plan more than you know in your heart of hearts you can accomplish.

Open Shelves

Open shelves in a kitchen require a bit more care regarding the selection and arrangement of items if you want things to look good and be accessible. But if you enjoy using the things you collect and love, you'll extend that joy when you arrange them for easy access.

Small, Good-looking Appliances

Black & Decker's Spacemaker Optima line of small appliances is the perfect way to maximize the space in your kitchen. These appliances are terrific looking and reasonably priced and if your kitchen isn't as up-to-date as you'd like, these products will make it function better without the expense of a remodeling job. And, if you're thinking about wedding gifts these are great for newlyweds who might have small kitchens. The coffeemaker, hideaway can opener, and horizontal toaster easily fasten under cabinets, freeing up counter space. The design has a white, clean, and sleek modern look.

ℰℐ Professional Stoves

If you're among the thousands of people putting in a new kitchen, remodeling an old kitchen, or just thinking about replacing your appliances, and you really enjoy cooking, you might like to consider a commercial-style stove.

These stainless steel beauties appear regularly in decorating magazines, and their industrial, chic good looks seem to promise a world of culinary delights unattainable with your ordinary range. Designed originally for restaurants only, many manufacturers of these powerful gas ranges are making them for homeowners. What attracts people to them is their superior high-heat performance and their hi-tech looks. When you have a professional range in your kitchen, no one doubts your cooking abilities. This, of course, could be a problem for those of us who can't do more than boil water and just want to foster an illusion. Be sure this is what you want because this particular illusion doesn't come cheap.

The Cost May Be Worth the Investment

Until recently few residential kitchens could accommodate the installation of these oversized units that require several inches of clearance on each side and back, let alone support its weight and adhere to safety requirements. However, due to the fact that the American Gas Association has certified that these ranges meet its stringent standards for safe home installation, there is considerable competition to capture the hearts of serious cooks in this country. With a price tag six times the cost of a regular gas range, it's not a lighthearted decision. However, you might decide it's the one item worth splurging on.

What Makes Them So Great?

If stove-top cooking is what you enjoy, this might be the range for you. While the ovens in professional ranges are excellent, most people buy them for their superior burners. High heat output is their big attraction. The burners are always gas, which provides immediate heat that can be adjusted exactly to your requirements. The flame coverage is even, and preheated pots and pans retain heat better. One of the biggest complaints has been that they do not maintain a gentle heat, the kind you can get when you want a slow simmer on your regular stove. Many manufacturers are working on this, however. Another thing to know is that not all professional ovens have a self-cleaning feature. This would definitely turn me off, but I'm not a cook.

Professional-style ovens are larger and more powerful than conventional ones. They are reliable, cook faster, and the heat is more consistent. If you aren't satisfied with four burners and would like six or eight, and you're thinking about a replacement, this might be the way to go. According to one kitchen designer, many people who have bought commercial stoves have confessed that they liked the look of them and figured the cooking would follow.

Good Things to Know

The current professional ranges are being designed for residential kitchens in that they fit snugly and safely right alongside kitchen counters. An overhead hood is required and there must be a certain amount of clearance from adjacent cabinets. The smallest size is about thirty inches wide and can run up to sixty-two inches. The most well-known manufacturers include Viking, Wolf, FiveStar, Thermador, and Garland. Wolf and Garland produce the most commercial-looking ranges. The others design products that are a bit more streamlined to fit into a standard depth countertop. Some models are available in colored enamel finishes and panels to cover the legs, but if you're looking for a professional range it would seem odd to want to disguise it.

Don't Forget the Extras

If you decide to throw caution to the wind and splurge on the pro-style range, keep in mind that you'll also have to factor in a hood and exhaust venting. Because they generate a great deal of heat, specially designed ventilation is necessary. Some manufacturers offer a venting unit designed for residential use. Some hoods also have optional features like a blower that automatically increases to high speed when it detects excess heat. If you're working with a professional kitchen designer, get as much information as you can to determine which item would be best for your situation. And too, keep in mind that a commercial range will last forever. If you're not planning to stay in your home for a long, long time you might not want to incur such an expense.

For more information about these stoves, the American Council for an Energy-Efficient Economy (ACEEE) publishes a book on major appliances. It can be ordered through bookstores. Or check on-line Web sites such as http://www.kitchen-bath.com/. This is Kitchen Net on-line help sponsored by Home Depot.

ℬ Bedrooms

Designers have made it extremely easy to create a completely coordinated look for the bedroom that's stylish and up-to-date without being terribly expensive. The bed and bath departments of stores like Macy's and Kmart offer Bed-In-A-Bag, the latest in designer coordinates. The basic ensemble includes sheets, pillowcases, shams, duvet cover, and bed skirt—in any size. No matter what style you prefer, whether it's a floral ensemble by Liz Claiborne, country ginghams by Martha Stewart, or the monochromatic scheme of Calvin Klein, to name a few, you can buy the whole thing in a bag. They take all the guesswork out of the job because they've done all the thinking for you.

A Riot of Color

If your style is lots of colorful florals you might choose a Liz Claiborne mix-and-match affair. The set comes with a bed skirt, pillow shams, pillowcases, duvet cover, and draperies or curtains to match. Along with this you'll also find wallpaper borders (not full rolls of wallpaper, although I'm sure these are also available in paint and wall-covering stores). In the bath arena you get the shower curtain, bath mat, wastebasket, towels, tissue-box cover, and toothbrush holder to match.

Do-It-Yourself Customizing

A friend of mine found her shower curtain wasn't long enough for her shower, so she solved the problem by buying an extra single sheet (you can get all the items separately) and making the bath curtain from this. She then added an inexpensive, clear shower-curtain liner. To save money she cut apart an extra pillow case and used the fabric to cover a plain wastebasket and tissue-box cover. She simply glued it on, and found they looked great for a lot less than it would have cost to buy the prefabricated ones.

Walls to Match

Choose one of the colors in a wallpaper border and sponge-paint the walls to give them a textured look. This is an excellent do-it-yourself project because it's one of the easiest decorative paint finishes. Or you can simply paint the walls in a color to match.

Country Style

Martha Stewart's gingham sets come in lovely pastel colors like pink, yellow, and aqua as well as a bold blue and white. I bought the blue and white set for my daughter's bedroom. This color scheme never goes out of style and always looks fresh, year after year, wherever it's used. To complete the country look, use white shutters for a crisp and carefree window treatment. Two inexpensive Chinese wicker trunks can then be spray-painted white and used as night tables. These are especially practical for extra storage space to hold linens in a guest room.

Alternative Styles

Other retailers that offer preselected, packaged bedding such as Laura Ashley sell fabrics by the yard, so you have many options, especially if you're a do-it-yourselfer and can do basic sewing. Look for inexpensive lamps and lamp shades in colors to match your bedding. Then, using the same color, paint a border all around the outside edge of the floor. You might find an inexpensive area carpet to complete the picture.

Victorian Style

If your taste runs more toward the all-white Victorian look that might include a canopy bed, look for a pretty white matelassé quilted cover, white ruffled sheets, and lace-edged curtains available from the *Country Curtains* catalog. Thrift shops are a good source of lace nightgowns and doilies that can be cut up and made into pillowcases. They are also good for making a skirt to go around an old kidney-shaped dressing table (these  vintage items are back in style) and another for a lace-edged skirt on the dressing-table stool.

There is nothing more lovely than using shades of white to create decorative effects on the walls, with the molding painted in a contrasting shade of cream. For pure luxury and elegance, drape a soft wool throw across the foot of the bed.

On the Walls

Beautifully framed botanical prints are lovely with any decorating style. I also like to hang a mirror in an interesting frame in a bedroom. Create a wall of framed family photographs to go with the mirror as part of a grouping.

For a Change

When decorating two bedrooms with Bed-In-A-Bag, a friend of mine bought two extra sheets in different colors. "It's a great way to change the look of the room from time to time," she explained. If you aren't hung up on the idea of really expensive sheets that cost as much as a down payment on a house, consider getting two or three sets of extra sheets that will go with the rest of the ensemble and you'll be all set. While they aren't the softest linens in the world, after a few washings with softener thrown in you won't know the difference.

Help for a Small Bedroom

If your bedroom is small and the ceiling is low, you can create the illusion of more space. Stripes give a room more height. This can be achieved with striped wallpaper or you can paint bold stripes in two contrasting colors to accentuate the height. The ceiling should be painted bright white.

❧ Personalizing Your Bedroom

A bedroom should be the place that is the most restful. Start with the most comfortable mattress set you can afford. If you can't afford another single item, this is where to splurge. A bed lasts a long time and you will spend many hours in it. The rest is easy. No matter what style appeals to you there's a way to achieve the look without spending a great deal of money. Most well-known designers have created a line of reasonably priced bed linens that sell through department and discount stores.

A Private Place

The concept of mixing and matching various colors and designs is back. Many decorators feel that bold wallpaper can be extremely attractive. Others prefer a monochromatic environment, finding the absence of color more restful. It's not necessary to have the bedroom match the decorating in the rest of the house. This is a private area where you can get away from it all. The important thing is that at the end of the day, this is the place you want to be. Use the things that make you feel good to look at. Everything should add to your well-being.

White Is Restful

Some people think of an all-white room as boring. Or they don't think of it as practical. Actually there are so many different shades of white that mixing them on different textures can be the perfect way to design a rich-looking room. Consider piling the bed with throw pillows in shades of vanilla, rosy white, linen, and eggshell. For the look of expensive sheets without the cost, buy plain white sheets and trim them with a lace or ribbon edging. Eyelet and lace edging are sold by the yard through fabric stores. They come in a variety of styles and widths and you can choose according to your taste and budget. This is also a good way to add trimming to plain pillowcases. A brocade or tapestry binding is a good way to dress up a plain white blanket as well.

Curtains

There are many options for window treat-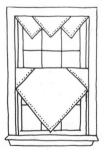ments, but since we're talking about getting great style for little money, the best way I know to achieve this is with plain white panels. You then have the option of trimming the edge with fabric to match your wallpaper, with embroidered ribbon, plain satin or grosgrain ribbon, or silk braid. Use any of these materials for tie-backs. I often use lace-edged linen napkins set on the diagonal over a curtain rod for a valance. No sewing involved!

To add a touch of color, paint window and door moldings with a subtle shade darker or lighter than the wall paint. Always use a semi- or high-gloss paint for these areas.

Accessories for High Impact

Country style is a comfortable look for a bedroom. It is warm and cozy and easy to live with. Braided rugs are cheap, practical, and come in all sizes and colors. If this style appeals to you, consider adding a rocking chair with a quilted pillow and a small quilted wall hanging as artwork. A strip of Shaker-style pegs along one wall adds to the look and is practical. A mother of two small boys says she can't imagine a room without pegs for hanging almost everything.

✸ The Guest Bedroom

Since most guest rooms are used infrequently, they tend to serve other needs when not occupied by a relative or friend. My guest room is usually filled with things for which there isn't enough room elsewhere. When my mother comes for a visit I simply tidy up and find temporary storage for the things I've piled on the bed or in the closet. Creating a pretty and comfortable guest room doesn't take a lot of money and it's quite satisfying to welcome a friend by providing a nice oasis no matter how long or short the visit. Since I live on a resort island, I know many people who entertain overnight guests in the summertime. Here's how some of them accommodate occasional guests.

Creative Use for a Closet

A friend of mine has just repainted her son's childhood bedroom. Now he comes to visit with a wife and baby. Since they never use the closet, but rather live out of a suitcase, she decided to make better use of that closet. When she replaced the twin bed with a double bed, it overwhelmed the space. So she removed the sliding closet doors and set the headboard of the double bed into the closet space. I suggested installing swing lamps on each side wall as well as a built-in shelf for a clock and other essentials. A painting on the wall over the bed finishes what is now a cozy little niche.

Keep It Simple

My guest room is rather small. In order to make it function efficiently I furnished it with a white wicker trunk placed at the end of the bed for holding blankets and towels. Guests use this to hold a suitcase. A small dresser is all that's needed, with a night table and lamps on each side of the bed. We then outfitted the closet with wire shelves, leaving just twelve inches for hanging clothes on one side. This makes it easy for guests to put clothes away, and between visits I use the shelves for storage.

The Bare Essentials

I asked several friends who have been guests or have guests often what a good guest bedroom should hold. From one, a full-length mirror on the back of the door. From another, a good reading lamp next to the bed. From my children, wall hooks so they don't have to hang clothes in the closet. Better yet, a chair over which to drape the clothes.

The bed is the most important element. It should have crisp new sheets, not the leftovers from years ago. A sumptuous down comforter is great, or a light blanket for summer. A pretty patchwork quilt is delightful. Lots of pillows, both for sitting up and reading in bed and for sleeping—with some soft and some firm so your guest can choose which is best for sleeping. European pillows with oversize shams are wonderful.

Nice Touches

Lavender sachets make unused drawers smell fresh. I also like to provide current newspapers next to the bed, the Chamber of Commerce booklet, a travel or style book about the area, and a map for a guest to peruse. Depending on the guest, I often take a few best-selling books out of the library for the eventuality of a rainy day.

For the Bathroom

A really good host stocks the guest bathroom with a basket of small bottles of shampoo, conditioner, hand cream, and suntan lotion. It's also nice to provide big fluffy towels, a soft rug by the shower, a wastebasket, exquisite soap in a porcelain soap dish, a new shower curtain, and a magazine holder filled with the latest issues.

Home Away from Home

Lately I've been staying in hotels in various cities while on business. It's given me a chance to assess what a really good home away from home should include. A magnifying mirror is a nice touch, a hair dryer, an iron, lots of pillows, fresh flowers in a vase, a writing pad with a container of pencils and pens, a few stamps, enough  hangers for dresses, shirts, and pants, a terry bathrobe, oversize towels (preferably white), a real blanket—not a bedspread posing as a comforter, a carafe with a glass for water, a basket of fresh fruit, real art on the walls, and a few artifacts on the table that make the room less sterile. I guess that's hoping for too much in a hotel, but certainly not in your own guest room. A telephone and phone book offer convenience.

Thing to Avoid

On the other end of the spectrum, I once stayed with friends for a night. The closet was so full of odd things like leftover Christmas wrapping paper and out-of-season clothes that there wasn't a hanger that didn't have three things already on it. Every inch of every surface was covered with stuff. The lamp next to the bed was bulbless and the pillows were flat as a pancake. The casualness of their household was appreciated in other areas of the house, but a guest bedroom should be a sanctuary.

Be Your Own Guest

Don't save pampering for your guests. Why not concentrate on your own bedroom and treat yourself as if you're the guest? Maybe it's time for new sheets, a new mattress, a new quilt, or a paint job. The great thing about updating a bedroom is that it can be relatively inexpensive to make it romantic, comfortable, and cozy. And if you're like me and never feel you're caught up on reading or corresponding, keep a basket next to the bed. Every time you find an article or a book you'd like to read, save it for when the weather turns nasty. Put a package of note cards, a pen, and stamps in the basket as well. If it's all there, you'll be more inclined to dig in.

ॐ Refurbishing an Old Bathroom

The bathroom can be an easy decorating project. It's small and it's therefore easy to make it look stylish without spending very much time or money. The basics are available in any price range and you can have fun with unusual colors for walls and accessories. Even if you play it safe and paint everything white, you can add color with the towels and change the scheme of things whenever you get bored. However, if you have an old bathroom that needs sprucing up, this can be done with paint, wallpaper, a wallpaper border, or wall-to-wall carpeting over unsightly linoleum.

The Formica Challenge

A woman wrote to ask me what she could do to update her bathroom that was covered with ugly Formica. She wanted to avoid a major renovation job. The first year she wallpapered over the Formica walls, but it didn't adhere well enough. If you have the same problem, the following will do the trick. Note: This project must be done on a dry day.

Use exterior house paint (we used stark white) and apply it over the Formica or wallpaper. This is an oil-base paint and must be left to dry for several days. Next use a glossy oil paint in a shade slightly darker than the base coat (we used linen white) and a natural sponge to soften the entire painted surface with a textured sponging. To do this, wear rubber gloves and plan to throw away the sponge and gloves when finished.

Once this is dry, sponge over the surface with a light gray paint in order to add a little color while softening and blending the textured sponging. Leave this to dry thoroughly. The end results will be stunning and best of all there will be no trace of the ugly and dated Formica bathroom underneath it all.

ℬ Bright White

When a bathroom is all white it looks clean, and bright and, often, larger than it really is. You can then introduce style with a little bit of color in each accessory you add.

Bath Towels

Towels are the most important accessory in a bathroom. You can choose any color towels for an all-white bathroom. However, most purists start with snow-white towels. This is one luxury everyone can afford, and the effect is exactly that . . . pure luxury. If you're choosing white towels, look for different textures and patterns in the all-white scheme. Large, fluffy white towels hanging on chrome or porcelain wall hooks will look great. If you have the space, hang a wooden strip of pegs along one wall for hanging towels and a terry-cloth robe. If the wood is stained dark walnut or cherry, it will cre-

ate a nice contrast between the white wall and the towels. These peg racks are available in most home centers, and can be found painted or in unfinished pine. The pine racks are ready for staining. Minwax wood stains come in a variety of wood colors and are easy to apply.

Fixtures

Probably the least expensive way to add high style to a bathroom is with drawer pulls and other fixtures. It's easy to replace old drawer handles with new, up-to-date ones. In fact, many catalogs are now featuring reproductions of old-fashioned fixtures that are good looking and very much in style. A new shower head and faucet handles can quickly and inexpensively bring an old bathroom into the next century.

Redo the Walls

If the walls of your bathroom are badly stained or in need of repair, consider covering them with white painted bead board. This is a tonque-in-groove paneling that you buy in strips or sheets from a lumberyard. The look is one often found in summer cottages and can be quite charming in a bathroom. Putting up bead board is an easy do-it-yourself project. Look for the precut panels from Georgia-Pacific Company.

Wallpaper Covers a Multitude of Sins

Wallpapering a bathroom is a small and inexpensive project, but the results can be dramatic. Be sure to choose vinyl paper, as it is easy to clean and is moisture-resistant. Wallpaper offers the opportunity to introduce color and pattern, even in an all-white room. For example, consider a striped pattern of one color and white. Or choose an overall pattern of green ivy on a white background. Add a fresh plant to a shelf, or hang a plant in a corner from the ceiling if shelf space is limited.

Little Things Count

All the little necessities one needs in a bathroom can be used to introduce color or texture. If you like the feel of an all-white bathroom without color, use natural colored baskets and pottery to hold brushes and cosmetics. Choose a white textured bathmat and a basketweave wastebasket. A  white pitcher filled with white flowers is a nice touch, or use a pitcher to hold other things. Terra-cotta clay pots that used to hold plants make wonderful containers for hair dryers, brushes, and shampoo bottles. Since you can find clay pots in all different sizes (and sometimes unusual shapes), they are extremely convenient containers.

Window Treatment

If privacy is a concern, you'll need a window treatment that can do the trick. However, the simpler, the better. A plain white fabric shade will soften the window area, give you privacy, and keep the all-white look intact. If you want to create the most light-reflective ambience in the room, hang sheer white fabric on the lower half of the window with a matching valance across the top of the window. It's quite easy to make a café curtain, because the only sewing requirement is a straight seam across the top, bottom, and sides of the fabric. Choose fabric with a pattern or texture in it. The amount of fabric you buy should measure two-and-a-half times the width of the window.

Wooden blinds give bathroom windows a crisp, contemporary look. They let you control the light and air circulation and come in a variety of colors. If you choose white, you can choose a contrasting color for the fabric strips that run down the front of each side.

Mirrors Visually Expand the Size of a Room

If the bathroom is cramped, cover the entire wall over the sink with a custom-cut mirror. This is not an expensive project. A good hardware or home center store will take your measurement and cut the mirror to size. You can hire someone to install the mirror or do it yourself. Home centers have kits with the appropriate glue for mounting the mirror to the wall. It helps if you have a partner to help with this project. An alternative would be to buy a large, framed mirror, or a grouping of small, interesting mirrors to hang individually on the wall.

Quick Fix for a Tired Bathroom

One of the easiest ways to spruce up a tired bathroom is with a fresh coat of glossy paint. If you want to do more, consider a faux finish over the fresh coat of paint. Simply mix a chosen color with glaze (found at all paint stores) and add texture with a ragging or sponging effect (see page 87–88). A stencil design is another way to freshen up tired walls. There are many precut stencils available in craft stores and home centers.

Lighting

An outdated light fixture can easily be replaced with track lighting to create a soft glow. If replacing light fixtures is too involved, consider adding a small tabletop lamp with a soft pink bulb. This is especially effective in a powder room where you don't want harsh lighting. The pink bulb is extremely flattering to both the room and people.

Flooring

Replace old vinyl or carpet with new peel-and-stick tile. The room is small, the tiles are inexpensive, and the project is a cinch to do yourself.

Relief from White

If you won't want to feel as though you're in a totally white box, paint the ceiling pale aqua or sky blue. This little detail will be a surprise addition to the room. Another surprise is that it provides just enough contrast to actually make the white seem even whiter.

Black and White

Introducing black into an all-white bathroom can result in a simple, contemporary look. A black-and-white color scheme can be achieved with a tiled floor. Four-inch square white tiles might be divided with two-inch square black tiles. Paint ceiling and floor molding glossy black for high contrast. Mix black and white towels on gleaming chrome towel bars for a contemporary look. Replace old cabinet knobs with shiny black ones. An inexpensive way to do this is by painting wooden knobs with a high gloss enamel. Add a checkerboard border around the room with small black and white tiles. Use them to create a splashboard above the sink, around the tub area, or as a frame around the windows.

A Little Luxury on the Floor

A slate floor adds luxury to the bathroom and is quite practical. The most typical colors are charcoal, green, and burgundy. Slate is sold like ceramic tiles and is precut to a standard ¼-inch thickness. It is installed much like ceramic tile. This material is not impervious to stains, so it's a good idea to apply a sealer. The look of a slate floor in an all-white bathroom is one of high style for low cost, considering the small space in which it will be installed.

Style for Pennies

Finally, if your budget doesn't allow for any sort of makeover, there's still hope. A colorful arrangement of silk flowers adds the perfect touch in an all-white bathroom. Replace a plastic shower curtain with one made of white terry cloth or textured fabric to warm things up. And for a no-sew curtain idea, attach clip-on curtain rings, evenly spaced across one long end of two terry-cloth hand towels. Hang them as café curtains. For full-length curtains, use bath towels and hang in the same way.

ℬ Small Spaces

Decorating small spaces often requires special consideration. It can be a real challenge to create delightful nooks and crannies that are totally unexpected when you come upon them.

For the Kitchen

If you have a small area in your kitchen or eating area, turn it into a pretty spot, with just a few accessories. For example, frame two or three botanical prints or a poster for the wall. Then hang a shelf under the framed prints to hold little pots of flowers or fresh herbs. I stenciled a window box with the word "herbs" and have a fresh indoor garden for snipping whenever I need a pinch of parsley, basil, or oregano.

A Pretty Laundry Room

Turn your laundry area into a delightful garden room. Start with a piece of fabric you love and use it to make a tailored valance for the laundry room window. Use a Duette blind to cover the window. Choose a precut stencil of flowers to grow up the wall under the window. Use an ivy vine stencil for around the outside of the window frame. Add real topiary trees on either side of the window. The room will be so cheerful that it will be hard to resist doing laundry more often.

Small Powder Rooms

I like to think of small powder rooms as art galleries. In my own downstairs half bath I have covered most of the walls with framed artwork from my artist friends. I also have a humorous postcard that was sent to us. It adds a touch of lightness. On both sides of the wall surrounding the sink mirror I have framed family photographs. A shelf holds small items that I think will interest guests who use this room from time to time. The window treatment is a simple one: The valance is made from putting lace-edged linen napkins set on the diagonal on a tension rod. No sewing needed. The bottom curtain is a café style, covering only the bottom half of the window. It is made from two embroidered linen towels found in a French flea market.

Quick and Easy Tips for Small Spaces

1. Use the area next to your fireplace to group like objects, both three-dimensional and small, framed artwork.

2. If you have a stairway with a landing, use this to hang small, framed photographs very low on the wall.

3. Frame vacation photos, notecards, prints, and artwork. If you have room to place knickknacks around, do this as well.

4. A hallway or entryway is perfect for decorating in a different way than you might do an entire room. Look at this area as setting the stage for what lies ahead. You might use a bright color paint if the rest of the house is more subdued. Or you might create an art gallery here, lining the walls with an interesting grouping. A mirror in a nice frame might be your starting point, then surround it with the art.

5. Don't think because the space is small it needs tiny objects or small artwork. A large piece of sculpture or painting might be perfect in this environment.

6. If you want the space to appear larger and calm, use a subdued color. However, a brilliant color can create excitement and provide decorative interest.

Have Fun

The fun in decorating small areas is in separating them from the rest of the house and concentrating on just that spot. In this way it won't be an overwhelming project and you can be a bit unrestrained, since if you want to change it at some point, it's not a big decision.

The Great
Outdoors

ℬ Deck Decor

I just received a news release with the following announcement, "Designer decks are the latest craze in home decorating." What does this mean? I wondered. Are decorators now specializing in designing decks? Hardly. But it does seem that many homeowners have already discovered furniture for outdoor living that's every bit as well designed as indoor furniture. Smith and Hawkins, long the respected name in quality garden tools, also showcases teak furniture for patios and decks. Brown Jordan is another respected name in solid, well-designed, and made-to-withstand-the-elements furniture.

However, more recently, outdoor furniture lines have added soft indoor-outdoor fabrics to make the deck and patio an extension of the living room, and just as stylish. While there's a wider variety being offered, stripes in hunter green and white are still the most popular, as this fabric blends well with the outdoors and is easy to live with.

Colorful Stains

Many homeowners are now using color to make the deck stand out from the crowd. The Flood Company, a maker of wood-care products says that whitewashing the deck with a solid color stain provides an elegant, upscale look. Contrast this with black wrought iron or red cedar furniture for a striking statement. Two-toning the deck is another dramatic option. For example, you might like white railings around a natural wood flooring or a floor stained gray. No need to wait a season or two for a new deck to weather gracefully. Now you can enjoy that silvery gray finish instantly with a stain. In this way you can help to waterproof and color at the same time.

Thompson's Water Seal, a respected name in this area, offers more than one hundred different stain colors. Flood's Solid Color Stain can be custom mixed just like paint, with dozens of colors ranging from white to gray to red and olive. Even neutrals can be fun to work with—you can add color in your fabrics and pots of flowers.

Flood's stain is abrasion-, chalk-, and mildew-resistant and offers convenient soap and water cleanup. They also have a product called Seasonite New Wood Treatment. If you'd like a free wood-care guide, call 1 (800) 356–6346, ext. 322 or visit their Web site at http://www.floodco.com.

Accessories

Outdoor lighting, flower boxes, trellises, and built-in benches are items that add mood and comfort outdoors. Mail-order catalogs are now offering all sorts of innovative lighting alternatives. Just when we find a problem, it seems there is a product to solve it. For example, there are all sorts of outdoor lanterns for any situation. There are hooks of major proportions for hanging a candle lantern from a porch ceiling, on the side of the house where you  might be dining, or another version for inserting into the ground around the patio, deck, or in the garden. These items are quite inexpensive and provide a means for transforming any outdoor area into a romantic dining oasis.

Candlelight

Outdoor electric lights won't do. They attract bugs and aren't conducive to setting a mood. I use candles of every size and especially like to put them in mason jars, glass globes, and vases that come from the florist. However, if you want a more decorator look, the hurricane globes with irregular bubbles in light green blown glass are great looking and inexpensive. Citronella candles are also necessary to keep away the bugs. The beautiful yellow color looks especially pretty in clear glass votive holders.

A Bit of Romance

I like to string fairy lights around the umbrella pole that goes into the center of my round table. In December we call them Christmas tree lights, but when used year-round, "fairy lights" or "moonbeams" seem much more appealing.

These tiny, clear glass strings of lights create just the right dots of sparkle around trees and fences and twirling up the umbrella pole. Many mail-order catalogs offer them ready-made for clipping onto the umbrella spokes over your outdoor table. If you do this yourself, you'll need lots and lots of sets for them to be effective.

Colorful Dining

Add more color with placemats and napkins as well as colorful plates and utensils. This is the place to have fun and try something different. While I prefer a monochromatic interior design, the greenery and colorful flowers we see in summer inspire me to extend this feeling to my deck. By the time I'm tired of all that color, the season is over and I'm happy to return to the calm contrast of a color-free home.

Preserving Wood on a New Deck

You should always put stain or water seal over pressure-treated lumber, say the experts at Thompson's Water Seal. In fact, you can apply their stain colors for instant aging and water seal in one step. Cape Cod Gray will give you a wonderful satiny gray color and protect the wood all at once. There are over one hundred colors available, but it's hard for me to imagine using any other than the gray on a deck. They also have natural wood colors and we used the honey stain for a warm wood color on our front porch. It looks great and the water beads right up each time it rains.

ℰℭ Outdoor Furniture

If you've just brought your patio chairs and tables up from the basement or out from the garage, you may have discovered that they don't look as fresh and new as you would like. If you want to invest a couple of hours, rather than several hundred dollars for new furniture, you can get a fresh new look with a bit of spray paint.

Decorator's Choice

Spray paint has improved over the years. It used to be available only in a few standard primary colors. But over the past couple of years, companies like Rust-Oleum and Krylon have developed a wide range of interesting colors. You're no longer limited to the standard primary red, white, and navy when choosing a color scheme. For example, Moss Green and Taupe, Colonial or Berry Red and a range of five different blues and three different hues of yellow make it easy to create an entirely new look for outdoor living.

Tips for Spray-Painting Like a Pro

The following are tips to make the job easier and longer lasting so you won't have to go through this process again next year.

1. Painting outdoors is ideal and it's best to do this when the temperature is above fifty degrees.

2. All loose rust and paint needs to be removed with a wire brush or sandpaper. Glossy surfaces need to be lightly sanded to keep the paint from "sliding" and allow for good bonding.

3. Built up dirt, oil, and grease can impair the paint's adhesion and cause peeling. Clean your furniture with soap and water and rinse thoroughly. Let dry completely.

4. For an extra long-lasting finish, you might use a primer before the top coat. There are different spray primers for different surfaces, such as rusty metal primer, clean metal primer, aluminum and wood primer.

5. Shake the aerosol can vigorously for about a minute after the mixing ball begins to rattle, and shake often during use. Probably the biggest mistake most people make when spray-painting is that they hold the can too close to the object and they don't keep moving it back and forth. The only way to get a really smooth finish without drips is by holding the can twelve to sixteen inches from the surface and spraying in a steady back-and-forth motion overlapping each stroke. Always keep the can in motion and apply two or more light coats a few minutes apart rather than one heavy coat.

6. Give the piece about two to four hours for drying to touch. It will take about five or six hours to dry for handling. But it's best to leave it drying overnight before using it.

7. When finished, turn the can upside down and spray until no paint comes out. This will clear the nozzle for the next use.

Decorative Touches

You don't have to confine yourself to a plain painted table or chairs. Once you've painted the surface, add a decorative stencil design to the backs of chairs or around the tabletop. Or use two coordinating colors to create an interesting piece of furniture. For example, paint the top of an occasional table with a cream color and use a shade of green such as teal or hunter for the rim and legs. Paint each of the chairs a different subtle color so they are coordinated. You might use a different natural shade for each one, such as Rust-Oleum's Satin, Shell, Flagstone, and Putty or contrast them by using Federal Blue on two chairs and Summer Straw on two. Rust-Oleum not only comes in spray cans but in cans for brush-on as well. And it isn't just for metal, but can be used to rejuvenate and protect your wicker or wooden furniture, too.

Painted Accessories for Outdoors

In Provence I found painted terra-cotta flower pots. Some were decorated with a simple painted border around the rim, others had a whitewashed look, and some were decorated with painted pastel stripes or dots. These are easy projects that anyone can do. Use your imagination with different paint colors to turn ordinary clay pots into fanciful planters. They don't have to be perfect. In fact, they seem more charming if they have a naive quality, almost as if a child had done them. Paint votive candleholders, metal lanterns, and all sorts of other outdoor accessories like window boxes and odd containers for holding plants around the patio.

A Fresh Start with Paint

If you don't want to do any creative painting but want to spruce up your outdoor space, give everything a fresh coat of white paint. You'll have a new look instantly. Every year, before I open my store for the season, I paint the floor with alternating wide stripes of blue and yellow. It has the look of a covered porch in a tropical setting. The walls are white and I have delicate wire plant stands in hunter green. A white slated porch swing hangs from the ceiling and we stenciled bright blue morning glories across the back. Everything looks fresh and new, even though it's just the same old floor and walls underneath it all. Now I'm ready for summer.

Remedy for Rusty Furniture

A customer told me that he had painted an outdoor swing and now it needed a new coat of paint. He wanted to change the color. I asked if it had been varnished, which it had. If you have a similar problem, the solution is to sand all surfaces lightly, then coat with Bin to seal it. Let this dry. Then apply outdoor paint in the color of your choice. Some brands of outdoor paint are now available in a satin finish, and the range of colors was created to match house trim and nature. Most outdoor paints can be used on wood, wicker, and metal.

ℬ Decorating with Pressed Flowers

Drying and pressing flowers from the garden is a great way to make things to give as gifts or to make your home more attractive. Right after they're in full bloom is the time to gather the petals, leaves, and grasses. You can preserve them and take the dried materials out to use when you're ready to turn them into something.

Flowers That Are Good for Pressing

I press rose petals, johnny-jump-ups, chrysanthemums, holly leaves, a variety of variegated leaves, stems, blades of grass, and a few lobelia blossoms in the hopes that they will retain their bright blue color. I often use a few geranium buds and leaves and the last of my leggy impatiens in the fall. I have a few ferny looking plants in my yard and I often use these for making Christmas cards.

How to Press

I do my pressing the old-fashioned way because it's the easiest. You simply lay the elements on a piece of paper toweling, cover with another piece, and place between books. Then pile books on top, or weight it down with bricks and leave it alone for about a week. Once when I was in a rush I put the pressed flowers between towels in the microwave. Someone told me you could do instant drying this way, but I wasn't convinced. The petals were flat and kept their color but they weren't as translucent as they get when left under books for several weeks. Sometimes

I press flowers between pages and put the books away and forget about them. Months later I find them and this always yields a nice dry-pressed variety of buds. So, if you can start

way before you need them you'll be gratified with a bounty of garden blossoms, albeit flat, dry ones, when you're ready to do some crafting. It's a great way to enjoy the fruits of the garden twice over.

Rose Petal Box

For most projects you'll need a variety of pressed material, craft glue, and something on which to arrange the items. One of my projects was a rose-petal covered box. Begin by painting a wooden box with latex or acrylic paint. Carefully arrange the petals on the box in a pleasing way. To glue the thin petals to the surface, dilute white craft glue like Elmer's Glue-All and brush it onto the box with a sponge brush. Tweezers are good for ease in handling delicate petals. You can use a pressed stem and leaves or cut these elements from paper and glue them in position to create a design on the box. Let this dry overnight. Protect with several coats of clear, quick-drying varnish. To finish the box, line it with pretty wrapping paper or wallpaper.

Framing a Wedding Picture

It's easy to personalize the way you frame a wedding photograph by decorating the matte with an array of tiny rose petals. Use a toothpick to make dots of glue all over the matte. Then carefully place the petals here and there on the glue. Cover with the glass and frame.

Making Creative Cards

Use your pressed material to create a nature scene on the front of a blank card. Once arranged, press a piece of clear Contact paper over the front of the card so it extends beyond the edges. Press down. If necessary, use a rolling pin or a drinking glass to roll over the Contact and remove all the air bubbles. Trim the edges so they are even with the card stock. You can make your own colorful cards with construction paper or poster board as well. Be sure to cut the cards so they fit in a standard-size envelope. For Christmas cards, arrange two holly leaves, for example, in the corner of the card. Use a red pen to draw the holly berries then write your message with a gold pen. Or, create a leaf border all around the card.

Kid's Photos and Drawings

Grandparents love to receive photographs of their grandchildren, or the kids' drawings as gifts. Decorate the cover of a photo album with pressed flowers and fill with photos you've taken throughout the year. Or, use the pressed flowers to decorate the edges of the photos on each page. For example, if you took pictures of the kids jumping in the leaves last fall, press a few fall leaves and add them to the pages of the photo album.

Natural Place Mats

You might like to make your own nature place mats with your pressed flowers. Use poster board cut to size. Then arrange the pressed flowers in a pleasing way and apply clear Contact paper overall. Turn over and apply Contact paper to the back as well. Trim all around edges.

Decorative Candles

I love to decorate plain candles with pressed flowers. As the wick burns down the center the flowers seem to glow from behind. This is a great way to create expensive-looking candles for pennies. Here's how it's done: Place a block of clear paraffin (available in hardware stores and supermarkets with canning supplies) in an empty coffee can. Put this in a pot of boiling water to melt. Carefully dip the candle into the hot liquid and remove. Immediately, while the paraffin is soft, use a tweezer to place the dried flowers around the outside of the candle. Let the candle cool for a minute or two and then quickly dip it into the melted paraffin again to coat the flowers and outside of the candle. Remove immediately and let cool until hard. Use a variety of colors to achieve different effects, or use all green on a white candle.

ℰ Garden Delights: Bringing in the Outdoors

There are many flowers that can be dried successfully and used for year-round arrangements. Dried flowers look especially beautiful when arranged in baskets. Some of the more colorful flowers are strawflowers and brilliant orange Chinese lanterns, which are quite lovely and will add color to a home all year long.

When the last petals of summer begin to fall to the ground it's time to make potpourri. Extend the life of your flowers by drying them for filling sachets. Lavender is my favorite scent and keeps closets, dresser drawers, and clothes smelling fresh. (See page 160).

Preserving the Scents

It's easy to preserve your garden by turning the petals and leaves into a delightful potpourri mixture. Pick petals when they are dry and at their blooming best. Cut off the heads and pull the petals off gently. You can mix them with dried herbs and geranium leaves.

To dry flowers, put a layer of petals in an airtight container and cover with salt. Add another layer and more salt and continue to layer in this way, stirring each time you add a new layer of petals. Add a pinch of cloves or allspice and cover tightly until ready to use. Then put it into a pretty basket or container. (See page 136 for more drying techniques.)

Everlasting Wreath

Many decorative herbs have a natural fragrance and are perfect for making an everlasting wreath to hang in your home. Everlastings are decorative flowers or foliage that air dry or preserve well. They can simply be hung upside down or dried in silica gel. In this way the natural col-

ors are preserved. Everlastings are most often air dried. To make a dried flower wreath you will need a grape vine or Styrofoam base. Strawflowers, baby's breath, herbs, and statice are especially good for drying and arranging on this kind of project. Using a hot glue gun run a few lines of glue on the wreath front and press Spanish moss into the glue to cover the base. Begin to add your dried flowers or herbs with spots of glue applied to the back of each piece. Then press firmly onto the moss. Cover all the moss in this way. Use larger pieces first, then add smaller pieces in between.

You can choose several colors or limit the colors to natural browns, beige, and green. Choose flowers of different shapes and sizes as well as types. Sprays of everlastings look especially good above a doorway or window. They might even make a nice valance to frame the top of your windows in place of a curtain.

Drying Roses

If you have a rose garden you might like to enjoy the roses long after they have given you pleasure in the garden and in cut arrangements in your home. These are best dried in silica gel, such as Flower-Dri, which is a finely powdered, sugarlike substance, in spite of the misleading fact that it's called gel. To dry the roses, first fill a container (I use a plastic shoe box) with an even layer of silica gel, one inch deep. Cut off all but one inch of the flower's stem. Place a double- or many-petaled flower faceup in the gel. Place single-petaled blossoms such as daisies facedown on top of the gel base. Flowers with long stalks should lie lengthwise in the container. Always include buds of roses and peonies in your drying collection. Place these horizontally in the gel.

Use a small spoon to cover the blossoms with gel, starting from the outer edges and working toward the center. Dust the crystals between the petals so the flowers will keep their shape during the drying process.

Cover the container with its lid or a sheet of aluminum foil taped in place. Don't leave the flowers in the gel for more than seven days or the petals will become too brittle. They are "done" if they feel crisp. If they are still limp, cover and leave them for another day or two. Lift the flower out and gently shake off the gel. To store the dried roses or peonies insert them in florist's foam. Or fill an egg carton with sand and insert a flower in each cup. To preserve your dried flowers until winter, simply put them in a storage box with a few mothballs and a few spoonfuls of the silica gel to keep humidity and bugs away.

Tips for Drying Flowers

1. Flowers picked to be air-dried should be as perfect as possible and moisture-free.

2. Flowers for drying should not be picked too early in the day. Let the warmth of the sun evaporate the dew first, and remove leaves from the stems to facilitate rapid drying.

3. The faster flowers dry the better they retain their colors.

4. Most flowers air-dry best when hung upside down.

5. Gather flowers in bunches and secure the stems with rubber bands. Hang upside down on a hook in a dry, dark area.

6. Dried materials can remain hanging indefinitely, as long as they are not hanging in a damp area.

7. To store flowers after they're dry, place them between layers of tissue paper in cardboard boxes.

Tidbits That Are Fun to Know

If you want to make an arrangement of flowers for a special person or occasion, you should know that the names of flowers have meanings. If, for example, you're throwing a bridal shower, you might like to decorate with baby's breath, which symbolizes purity of heart. For a baby shower, fill little pitchers and teacups with buttercups because they suggest a childish cheerfulness. If your party is meant to introduce two people unlikely to get together without you, fill the room with peonies and roses. The first suggests bashful, the second represents love. An anniversary celebration might be enhanced with sunflowers and verbena, the first suggesting loyalty, the second fidelity. If you want to soothe away sorrow, do it with a vase filled with yarrow.

Say It with Veggies

If your fresh items come more from the supermarket than the garden, you might like to create an all-green arrangement with items like Granny Smith apples, heads of cabbage, grapes, long green peppers, leeks, and a few branches of green leafy vegetables all grouped in a salad bowl.

Details That Make a Difference

✑ Finishing Touches

There are hundreds of quick and easy ideas for brightening small areas of your house, making things cozier, or adding much needed storage space. These finishing touches are like icing on the cake. You can live without them, but they will make your home look and feel better.

A Bright Spot

Paint small occasional knickknack shelves a bright color. Then, using double-faced tape, add a front edge of lace, rickrack, ribbon, or paper doily trim. Arrange the shelf with brightly colored mugs, plates, and pitchers filled with flowers.

From Plain to Fancy

It's easy to take plain glass apothecary jars or an inexpensive white pitcher and turn them into works of art. Use permanent paint

and a cotton ball to apply an overall polka-dot design on the items. Then line the jars on a windowsill in sunlight and fill with flowers, or use to hold wooden spoons in the kitchen, or cotton balls and makeup brushes in the bathroom.

Add Storage Space

Mount wooden cubes (available in bed and bath stores or shops selling storage units) on the bathroom wall to create extra space for holding towels and personal items. If you have a blank wall area, mount a closet pole for hanging lots of towels. If you have unused space above the toilet, hang a shelf for extra towels.

For the Bedroom

Make a bed coverlet in a patchwork pattern by stitching large cotton or linen napkins together. Alternate solids and prints, or checks and florals in the colors of your choice.

Jazz Up a Plain Dresser

Make an ordinary dresser look up-to-date with interesting new drawer pulls. Paint oversize, unfinished wooden knobs in bright primary colors for a child's dresser.

For the Bathroom

Make a brightly patterned shower curtain. It's one of the easiest sewing projects and will instantly change the look of this room. No sewing skills? Use a single bedsheet with a border design. Add grommets or clip-on curtain rings evenly spaced across the top edge. The grommets and the tool for setting them come in a package at fabric and sewing stores, home centers, and paint and hardware stores.

Dressing Up

Add a flower wallpaper border around a door frame, window, or eating area in the kitchen. Use prepasted paper for greatest ease.

Fresh Herbs

Start an herb garden in a pretty pot on your kitchen counter. Or force bulbs to grow indoors. Every day brings new surprises. This tiny finishing touch is amazingly effective.

Try a New Color

Paint the wood trim in one room with an unusual color you've always been attracted to. Try one of the new berry colors, deep green, or bright coral.

Around the Fireplace

If you have a fireplace, move all the furniture closer to this area of the room. If your sofa is against the wall, pull it away, or place it next to the fireplace. If your coffee table is large, exchange it with a small occasional table in front of the fireplace so the sofa can fit closer. Even if the table is higher than your coffee table it will work.

Making Arrangements

Cover an occasional table with a quilt that goes right to the floor. Then make an arrangement of "comfort" things on top. This might include a grouping of framed photographs, a lamp, a pile of books, and a small potted plant. Controlled clutter makes a room warm and cozy, especially during the winter.

Tablecovers Made Easy

If you don't have a quilt for a table, you might like to know you can buy prequilted fabric to make one. This is a good weekend project. To make a round tablecover, measure from the center of the table to the floor. Double this amount and add four inches. This is both the length and width of the fabric you'll need to buy. Since fabric usually comes forty-five inches wide, you'll probably need two or three lengths to stitch together. Next, find the center of the fabric and mark with a pin. Cut a length of string from that point to the outer edge of the fabric and attach a pencil to the end. Hold the pencil perpendicular and draw a circle around the outer edge of the fabric. Cut out and hem. Finish the edge with double-fold hem binding, or turn the edges under and stitch around.

Change the Arrangement

Move things around and the room will look different. For example, exchange the things on a table with those on a shelf. Move things to a different room. Rearrange the furniture. Change lamps for a different lighting perspective.

Getting Ideas

Look through a bunch of home furnishings catalogs, magazines, and books. Jot down ideas of things you'd like to do, even if in your heart of hearts you know you probably won't. In book publishing they have a name for style books. They call them "dream books." So when the snow is falling and the temperature drops, gather the material around you, snuggle into your new cozy environment, and dream about the projects you may or may not do. Who knows, you just might.

ॐ Favorite Things

Most decorating magazines have a page that represents the editor's favorite things. These items are usually related in some way to new products on the market. Over the years I've accumulated a few favorite things without which I can't set a table, decorate for the holidays, arrange furniture, do a tablescape or whatever else needs attention in my home.

Accessorizing with Character

Everyone has their stable of staples. It might be an inherited lace-edged linen tablecloth, ornate silverware, a lovely tea set, or a needlepoint pillow. Over the years I've styled many photographs for our books and for decorating magazines. This forces one to accumulate many items that always add character, just the right color, or a much needed accent to a photo shoot. For this purpose, I lug home yellow and blue dishes from Provence, worn lace pillowcases, and an assortment of pottery from trips. I also use these items as often as possible because I only get what I love. Everyone has a few things that make them happy to look at because they have a personal meaning. It might be a gift you received from a close friend, a souvenir you bought while on vacation, or something you saved from your childhood. When displayed, these are the things that add character to a room, because they have a special meaning.

Setting a Lovely Table

When I'm having company I count on my ornate silverware to dress up the plain inexpensive white dishes I favor. My grandmother's cranberry-glass water goblets always do the elegant trick instantly. Don't keep your best things wrapped away for another generation to discover and enjoy. Use it all now.

Collections

Empty nesters often move from a large family home to a smaller house or apartment. After years of collecting it's time to weed out. If you're in this situation you may have too many wonderful items to use all at once. Play house and spread everything about, then carefully choose those things that relate in size, color, texture, and shape and make "tablescapes" in each room. This seems a less daunting assignment than decorating from scratch. These final touches make a room come alive and feel like home.

Cozy Up for Winter

Winter is a good time to bring out the comfort things. If your house is basically white, for example, color can come from collections giving the room different personalities. All you have to do is shift the collectibles to do this. If you have a variety of blue and white porcelain, line it along the living room mantel. Brightly colored majolica will give another feeling to a room, as will a colorful quilt hanging on a wall, draped over a sofa, used as a tablecloth, or on the bed. All these things add character without great expense.

Add an Element of Surprise

When arranging things it's always fun to add an element of surprise. For example, plain white drapes might be lined with a colorful floral print. When they're tied back, the color is revealed. Wallpaper where it isn't expected, such as in a closet or tiny powder room, can be quite charming. Paint the inside of your hall closet a bright cheerful color and add solid brass hooks for practicality. Or, create a photo gallery inside the closet door. A small powder room is the perfect place for a gallery of collectibles like folk art, unusual signs, and framed postcards.

Finishing Touches for an Older Home

My friend Linda lives in an early Nantucket house. The rooms are small and intimate and the house has been restored beautifully. When painting the living room she decided to texture the walls with ragging in a pale peach-color paint. She then used a precut stencil design that she especially liked to create a delicate border around the ceiling line. The mantel and wood surrounding the fireplace is painted in the original dark green color, which adds a nice contrast. The room is furnished sparsely but comfortably and it is at once warm, inviting, and up-to-date without spoiling the integrity of the original house.

Bring the Outdoors Indoors

Outdoor furniture and garden urns are unexpected when found inside, and they can be used in creative ways. Bring the garden indoors for winter to keep a room fresh and bright throughout the gloomy, gray days. I favor one oversized container with a small tree or a large urn holding sprawling ivy. In this way you don't have to forsake the plants you love due to a change of season.

New Things

Even if you don't have a collection of things you love, it's easy to acquire decorative accessories to enhance your home. When furnishing a home, sometimes the last things you're thinking about are the finishing touches. It can be fun to give yourself a little assignment. For example, pick an amount of money you can afford to spend frivolously at a particular time. Then without any preconceived idea, go through a housewares department shopping for any small things that you're immediately attracted to. Don't hesitate. Just buy them. The instant appeal of the item is all that matters. Don't overanalyze or agonize over the purchase. Trust your instincts and it will look great.

Using Things in Unexpected Ways

I have a set of old metal kitchen canisters that are totally useless for their original intent. They're rusty inside and the paint has faded on the outside. However, the green paint and floral decals are pure vintage 1940s and I like the look. At first I used them to hold odds and ends in my office, but this proved impractical. Then I lined them up in progressive size on a shelf in our studio. They looked good but took up much needed shelf space. Finally I filled each with a pink geranium plant and put them on tables around my deck. They look great and they have a use. If you have something you love and can't find a way to display it, keep trying new ways to use it until it works for you.

℘ Decorative Ribbons

Ribbons are one of the best inventions on earth. For relatively little money one can create wonders with ribbons. Even the most mundane gift, like a pair of socks, can be transformed into something special when wrapped in layers of tissue tied with an extravagant ribbon bow. But ribbons have more uses than for wrapping packages. They are wonderful accents for all sorts of decorative touches in your home, especially during the holidays.

French Style

My favorite is the French wire-
edged wide taffeta ribbon that has
become quite accessible in the last
few years. It used to be available
only through specialty shops or
sold in large quantity to designers
for store displays. Now it can be
found in all notions and craft stores

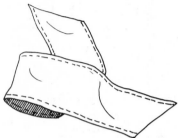

and in a wide variety of materials. I like the gold and silver
metallics, the deep green and cranberry red taffeta, the gold and silver netting, and the sheer organzas in pale pastel colors. White satin
ribbon is another favorite.

Ribbon Magic

Vogue Patterns publishes several beautifully illustrated booklets
on using ribbons for crafting. One project shows how to use green
organdy ribbons to decorate a napkin and napkin ring. The result
will make any table setting exquisite. Depending on the color you
choose, you can create a pretty setting for the holidays, a birthday
party, or Easter dinner.

To do this project you'll need 90 inches of 25 mm. pale green
organdy for each napkin and 63 inches of ribbon for the napkin
ring. You'll also need a wooden or plastic napkin ring, a 20-inch-
square linen or cotton napkin with hemstitching, an embroidery
needle, and a hot glue gun (Elmer's will do if you don't have the glue
gun).

1. Use the entire length of ribbon for the napkin and thread it
through an embroidery needle (which has a large enough eye to do
this).

2. Leaving about a 10-inch tail at the beginning, start at one
corner and, on the right side of the napkin, weave the ribbon
through the hemstitching going over 9 stitches and under 4 stitches.

3. Continue weaving around the napkin. Tie the ends of the
ribbon in a bow at the corner. Trim ends of ribbon diagonally.

To make the napkin ring, cut a 22-inch length of the ribbon and set aside.

1. Secure the beginning end of the remaining ribbon on the inside of the napkin ring with a hot glue gun or a spot of white glue.

2. Wrap the ribbon around the napkin ring overlapping edges slightly. When you get to the end, glue to the inside of the ring.

3. Take the remaining ribbon, which was set aside, and tie it around the ring. Tie in a bow. Leave ends as streamers.

Decorative Touches for the Holidays

Use this ribbon weaving technique to dress up your holiday table. Simply choose the ribbons in deep green and burgundy. Create a coordinating ribbon-trimmed tablecloth or place mats. Or trim plain items such as pillowcases and guest towels. To figure the amount of ribbon needed, measure the total perimeter of the item you want to trim. Add up all sides and add approximately twenty inches to the measurement for the bow.

Personalize Christmas Stockings

Personalize Christmas stockings for your family with luscious velvet, organdy, embroidered, and taffeta ribbons. It's easy to make an elegant stocking that will become an heirloom. You'll need: ½ yard of velvet or velveteen, a piece of quilt batting 16 by 22 inches, and 1½ yards of three or four different ribbons in different widths to go around the cuff. Tiny gold beads can be a wonderful added decoration, if desired.

1. Use an old Christmas stocking to cut out a pattern. With right sides of fabric facing, cut out two velvet stockings and two batting stocking pieces.

2. From the velvet, cut a cuff 11 inches long by 16 inches wide.

3. Pin batting to wrong sides of velvet stockings.

4. With right sides together, stitch stockings together using a ¼-inch seam. Leave upper edge open.

5. Turn stocking right side out. Pin or baste raw edges together.

To make the cuff:

1. With right sides facing, fold cuff in half, bringing 11-inch edges together.

2. Stitch with a ¼-inch seam and press seam open.

3. Fold cuff again with wrong sides facing. Pin or baste raw edges together.

4. Beginning about a ½ inch from the folded edge, pin thin ribbon around the cuff, turning in ends at seam. Stitch along edges.

5. Attach a wide ribbon and another row of the narrow ribbon to the cuff in the same way.

6. Sew a row of gold beads along the outer edges of the applied trims, if desired, about ½ inch apart.

To finish:

1. Turn cuff so ribbon trim is on inside. Insert cuff into the stocking, and with raw edges even, sew cuff to stocking.

2. Fold the cuff over the top of the stocking for ribbon trim to show.

3. Sew a band of ribbon inside stocking along edge of seam where cuff and stocking join. If desired, you can sew gold beads ½ inch apart along upper edge of ribbon where cuff and stocking join.

4. Use organdy or embroidered ribbon to make a bow and tack to the front of the cuff.

5. Use a pretty ribbon or gold cord to make a hanging loop. Or, cut 16 inches of gold metallic ribbon and fold in half. Sew tiny gold beads to it, ½ inch apart. Fold in half again and tack securely to the back edge of stocking to create a hanging loop.

6. Use another length of gold metallic ribbon to form a four-loop bow. Tack in the middle to secure and attach to the stocking over the hanging loop, where it attaches to the stocking. Cover tacking with beads if desired.

Curtain Tie-Backs

Wide ribbons can be used to perk up plain curtain panels. Use them as tie-backs and you'll have added a touch of color and personality that is easy to change when you want a different look. Pull the panel back to where you think it looks best, then hold the ribbon around the fabric at this point to see if this looks right. If so, cut the ribbon so it is long enough to go around the curtain and leave enough at each end for folding under ¼ inch. Cut the ribbon and press the raw edges under. Then, using a clip-on ring (available in home centers), fasten one to the center of the ends so you can attach it to a hook in the wall on both sides of your window. If you want to add more decoration, cut enough ribbon to make fat bows with a few inches for streamers and attach to each side of the tie-backs where they meet the side of the window. You can either hook the bow over the tie-back hook or pin in place. This creates a nice finished look.

ℬ Pillows

What is it about throw pillows? We always seem to need more of them. We're always attracted to them. They perfectly combine texture, color, and pattern.

If, for example, you're attracted to the color red, you don't have to paint the room, re-cover the sofa, or make a major purchase in order to bring the color in. A decorative pillow does the trick instantly and relatively inexpensively.

Combining Prints and Colors

Pillows are an excellent way to add a small dose of a contrasting color. Pick up the accent color from the other pillows, something else in the room like the carpet, drapes, or a china pattern. In this way, if you have a beautiful vase or painted furniture piece, you can tie in the colors found in the hard furnishing with the soft furnishing.

Combining colors and prints is a very satisfying challenge. For example, if you have a blue and white room you might add a green or yellow floral print with a few pillows in a checked fabric.

If your room is monochromatic, add a bunch of pillows in the colors found in nature, such as rust, green, beige, burnt orange, and shades of brown. Mix in some subtle prints such as beige-and-white-striped patterns.

Change with the Seasons

Use pillows to introduce a new color scheme when your room needs a fresh look. Change it for the seasons by using light flowery chintz for spring or summer, then remove the pillow covers and replace them with fall or winter linen or wool in subdued or tapestry hues.

Making Pillows Is Easy

It's easy to make your own pillow covers and you'll be able to get the look you want for pennies. Often the simplest combination works the best. I am often asked how I decide what to put together to make a patchwork pillow, for example. Or, how do I decide what fabric to use for the piping and the backing, which I often contrast with the main fabric of the pillow.

First I choose the colors. Then I try to combine large and small patterns. A large yellow-and-white check might look good with a small blue-and-white check. Or, I use a small checked fabric in a color found in the main fabric for the backing of a printed pillow.

When I design pillows that will be used together on a sofa, for example, I especially like to make each one slightly different, but using something on each one to tie them together. For example, when making pillows with blue and yellow fabric, I use one print to make the piping that will edge the pillow made from a contrasting print. Then I choose another fabric for the back of the pillow. I might use a small butterscotch check for the back of a blue-and-yellow-printed front. Then I would use the yellow check for the piping on another blue floral print. In this way, when the pillows are grouped together on a sofa, each is slightly different but they are united. It is more interesting than if all the pillows were exactly the same.

What Size Pillows Are Best?

Choosing sizes is another consideration. A young woman just furnishing her first home asked me how many pillows and what sizes are appropriate for an average size sofa.

I make pillows that are sixteen and eighteen inches and throw a fourteen-inch pillow against one of these. I call the little ones "filler" pillows. They add a spot of color where needed and the size is good for the small of the  back. For large sofas I like one or two oversize pillows, about twenty-two inches, that are quite soft and squooshy.

The Right Mix

Mixing patterns can give a room excitement, or make it look chaotic. The trick is to edit down everything else. If you have a patterned rug and fabric in the room, keep the walls free of wallpaper or use a small, overall, repeat pattern. Carefully select and arrange just a few collectibles on a table. Or, just a vase of cut flowers can be fresh and lovely.

Different Styles for Different Rooms

Pillows for the living room can be more tailored than for the bedroom. You can never have too many pillows on a bed. I mix large European-size pillows with standard or square ones. Mix tailored and ruffled. In my white bedroom I mix different shades of vanilla and shell so that everything isn't hospital white. Pillows of different sizes with one that is very delicate and feminine make a bed sumptuous and inviting.

The Three C's

Always remember the three C's when decorating for summer, especially for the porch, deck, or patio. Keep it Casual, Comfortable, and Carefree. Adding soft pillows with washable covers to a sofa or chairs will do the trick. Your living space, whether indoors or out, will be transformed instantly.

Creating a Mood

There are many inexpensive ways to add just the right mood to a room. It might be a fresh bouquet of flowers, music playing softly in the background, candlelight, soft lighting, the warm smells of food simmering on the stove, scented potpourri, even carefully arranged piles of books. Whatever the mood you're seeking, there is something you can do to enhance that feeling.

ଓ Flowers

As a decorative accessory, nothing perks up a room for so little money as fresh cut flowers. A clear glass vase filled with garden flowers, a few books, and perhaps a pretty plate on the coffee table will give the room personality. If you have a bare corner, fill it with a flowering plant. A large ficus or hibiscus is all you need to make a living room inviting.

The Current Look

Just as with other furnishings, the look of flowers changes style from time to time. Right now the fashionable approach is minimalism. With this attitude flowers should all be cut exactly the same length and not mixed. A pure bouquet of one flower is preferable to a mixed bunch. Wildflowers make a country statement while the pristine lily is more formal and au courant. No leaves, please! would be the dictate of the purists. Clear, heavy, cut-glass vases win out over ceramic pitchers and crocks, or anything fancy.

Arranging

Once arranged, edit your bouquets. A simple bud in the bathroom, or flowers of one color on the dining room table, is the way to go. Strip leaves. One hydrangea bundle is the absolutely perfect accessory, especially in a blue room. Choose flowers that reflect a color in the room. Or, use a bunch of flowers in one color as an accent in a neutral room. I once visited an apartment where everything was white and every table held a clear glass vase of red tulips. It was sensational. This is especially nice in the dead of winter or for the holidays. It's very clean looking.

Changing the Look of a Room

It's easy to change the look of a room by changing the floral arrangements. While summertime suggests casual arrangements such as wildflowers in baskets, roses in pitchers, cosmos and daisies in country crocks, the fall colors give rooms a transitional look. Just as we move from light-colored clothing to darker, more subdued colors for fall and winter, you can do this with your decorating. Without changing one single piece of furniture you can create a fresh new look with cut flowers.

Creative Ways with Plants

In spring fill a large basket with pots of red, yellow, and orange primroses. Then surround them with Spanish moss to give the arrangement uniformity. The primroses are often available in the grocery store and the moss is available at garden centers. In the fall, fill the basket with a golden chrysanthemum plant.  One of my favorite ways to decorate for autumn is to fill a child's wagon with red, yellow, and orange chrysanthemum plants and put it on the deck or beside the front door. At yard sales look for interesting containers that might be good plant holders. For example, for the Fourth of July I use a collection of old-fashioned white enamel cooking pots with painted red rims for holding red geranium plants. My bicycle basket is perfect for holding trailing ivy on the inside of the front door because the basket is flat across the back. In summer I fill it with pink and white impatiens and put it on the outside of the door.

Good Buys

Flowers are quite reasonably priced when purchased in the grocery store. It is here that I find small rose plants, cut flowers, and seasonal plants as well as hanging baskets of flowers. I've found that carnations are always available in white, pink, and red and they last longer than most cut flowers. They  smell good, they're delicate and look wonderful in tall and short vases, and they are generally less expensive than most other cut flowers. In other words, they are a good deal.

ℰℴ Sweet Scents

There are subtle things that add something extra special to a home. One of those things is scent. It might be the smell of good cooking every time one enters your kitchen or it might be the smell of fresh flowers. A linen closet or powder room filled with the scent of potpourri is a treat. It's like adding perfume once you're dressed to go out.

The Colors of Lavender

The house we rented in Provence was a restored seventeenth-century stone structure built into the side of a steep hillside. The view from our terrace was spectacular, even in the overcast mist that unfortunately lay about us almost continuously. But it was that time of year when the mostly green landscape is dotted with exquisite patches of purple. Rows and rows of lavender are planted with a strict linear geometry in fields that become a sea of purple spiky globes that seem to march on forever. By mid-July this exquisitely beautiful plant dominates the area both in sight and smell. Lavender plants are available in garden centers, and a fresh lavender plant is the perfect accent in any room. It is beautiful to look at and adds a wonderful subtle scent to the air. Dried stalks of lavender are equally beautiful and make a wonderful bouquet in a bedroom or bathroom.

Uses for Lavender

All the markets and street fairs in southern France are filled with lavender products: lavender sachets, lavender soaps, lavender honey, lavender vinegars, lavender tea, lavender body cream, and dried bunches of the deliciously heady herb. You can buy lavender sachets in boutiques in America or loose dried lavender from garden centers to make your own. I use it to fill a basket lined with a lace-edged linen napkin for the purpose of keeping my bathrooms and closets well scented and must-free. Use a lace-edged  hanky to make a sachet bundle. Pour a small amount in the center of the hanky, draw up the corners, and tie with a ribbon a few inches down.

Lavender is also a deterrent to mildew in closets. Place small bowls of lavender inside the cabinets and drawers and in the corners of the room. It not only keeps away that awful insidious mildew smell, it will give your home a lovely, subtle, and fresh scent that isn't cloyingly icky sweet the way some potpourri can be. Put some inside shoes that aren't worn often. It will keep mildew from creeping in and your feet might even seem happier.

Essence of lavender has exhaustive uses, from cleaning skinned knees to adding a freshness to the water we use to clean our floors. It might be noted that French women add lavender to their cleaning water because it has been known to repel scorpions. Fortunately we have no such need, but it certainly can't hurt to try it for repelling some of our own annoying summer bugs. Who knows, we may find our very own remedies or excuses for using lavender. It has to be better for the spirit than ammonia.

Lavender Is Restful

A drop of lavender oil in the rinse cycle when washing sheets has been known to induce a most restful night's sleep. For more exotic uses less drastic than repelling scorpions, tuck lavender soap between your linens, add lavender oil to your bath, clear a stuffy head by inhaling the steam from lavender-infused boiling water, and spread lavender honey on your morning toast to have with your lavender tea.

Drying Lavender

Can there be anything nicer than a basket filled with fresh lavender? The wonderful thing is, it lasts forever. After enjoying it fresh in a vase, tie a bundle together with twine and hang it upside down in a dark cool place, like the basement, for drying. Once dry, arrange the stalks in a basket and you can keep it indefinitely. To make your own potpourri add a drop or two of lavender oil to the buds and toss in a bowl. If you place a bowl of lavender in the closet or on the bathroom sink, toss it from time to time to release and rejuvenate the scent. And if you love the colors of the dark purple flowers with the deep green stalks, consider this your inspiration for a whole new decorating scheme. You could come to love it almost as much as the wonderful yellow and blue we usually identify with Provence.

❧ The Romance of Candlelight

Candles are an easy, affordable, and delightful way to change or enhance every room for whatever reason and in every season. In fact, all it takes to make an evening special is lots of candles. It's amazing how this sort of lighting instantly changes the mood. And if you still can't afford the more expensive lamps you've been dying to buy, make the most of candlelight whenever you entertain. It's all about ambience not individual things.

For the Holidays

Bring warmth and sparkle into your home from Christmas through the New Year with candlelight. Create a holiday mood from the moment your guests come through the front door by covering the surface of a table with different candles in all sizes and styles—votives, candlesticks, and hurricanes. Line fat red and green candles along the mantel and surround with freshly cut pine branches.

To create spots of holiday cheer, use bayberry and cranberry candles here and there on tables, mantel, kitchen counter, bathroom sink. They give off a nice seasonal scent. Place a fat candle in a larger clear glass bowl, vase, or other container. Fill partway with water and insert sprigs of holly leaves and berries all around.

Unusual Candle Holders

I have a collection of old wooden thread spools that I use to hold candles on my coffee table. They're grouped together and I light them every night just as it begins to get dark outside. The reflection of candlelight in the darkened windowpanes makes the panes appear cheerful rather than foreboding.

Put a Glow Here and There

You can have all the atmosphere and none of the fuss by using several pillar candles of various heights in your fireplace. Or, brighten hallways and stairways with candle wall sconces. Group two or three glass votive holders on your vanity and fill them with pure white or pale pastel aromatic candles.

For the Table

Make a centerpiece of candlelight surrounded by a ring of fresh flowers. To do this, soak a foam wreath in water and place on a dish or plate. Insert fresh flowers to create a full, flowering, rounded mass of blooms. Red roses with sprigs of baby's breath would make a delightful centerpiece for your Christmas or Valentine dinner table. Insert a votive holder and candle in the center, or if there's room, add several votives or fat candles of varying heights on the plate. If so many roses are beyond your budget, you can get the same look with red carnations for a fifth of the price, and it will last longer. Or simply cut greens from the yard and create an all green wreath with white candles in the center. For a holiday table add some sparkle with small silver tree balls here and there on the greenery. Or add pinecones, small lady's apples, or kumquats and nuts.

For the Bedroom

Don't wait for a special occasion to indulge in the simple pleasure of candlelight in the bedroom. Start a good habit by treating yourself to your favorite scented candle. And there's nothing more spiritually uplifting than spending an hour soaking in a tub on a cold Sunday afternoon, surrounded by candlelight. It's these simple pleasures within our homes that make us feel good. Creating a candlelight environment is a splendid beginning. Every evening when you come home from work, or end the chores of the day, light all the candles and enjoy being at home. You can't overdo a good thing.

For Gifts

A box of white dripless tapers and a few fat beeswax candles make wonderful gifts no matter the occasion or time of year. For a wedding gift, team them with a wonderful pair of glass candlesticks. For a birthday gift, buy ceramic candlesticks in a color to match his or her decor. For an anniversary, give candlesticks in the spirit of the year. Silver candlesticks or those made of china or glass, for example. Everyone appreciates them. And while you're at it, always take stock of your own cupboard to be sure you never run out of white candles in two sizes.

ℬ Lighting

Lighting is always the last consideration when remodeling or decorating a room. But it can be the most important finishing element in a successful completion. In fact, lighting can change the mood of a room and create an ambience that is appropriate for the activities done in that room. When the lighting is all wrong, too harsh or not bright enough, it is immediately apparent and bothersome.

A Welcoming Sight

It is so easy to create ambience with a single lamp. Lamplight in a room provides a warm and welcoming presence. A soft light left on in a front hallway for those not yet home is such a loving gesture. It exudes a feeling of coziness.

Table Lamps Are in Style

There was a time when decorating took a turn toward a more modern view with regard to lighting fixtures. Suddenly table lamps were old-fashioned and everyone wanted track lighting or recessed ceiling lights. However, I'm happy to say that the table lamp is once again quite in vogue and that it serves more than the purpose of providing light for doing specific tasks. In fact lamps are very much a fashion accessory in the world of interior design. When a lamp goes out of style, often all it needs is a new shade and it will fit right in again.

Creating a Mood with Lighting

Unlike other types of lighting, a table lamp is a wonderful way to light a room. We can create soft seductive lighting or intense lighting wherever we need it. We can also move a table lamp around to get just the effect we want, both from the lighting and from the lamp itself, as a decorative accessory. There are hundreds of styles and designs for any decor. Best of all, one doesn't need an electrician to install a table lamp.

Finding the Right Lamp

Until recently it was almost impossible to find well-designed lamps that didn't cost a fortune. Today, many home furnishings catalogs offer a variety of lamps in different styles for all situations.

Lampshades Are Important

Lampshades are another key consideration when buying or refurbishing a lamp. Proportion is everything. As a rule, a lampshade's vertical measurement should exceed the diameter of the top rim of the shade, but not by an enormous amount. For small, spindly lamps, it's best to use smallish shades.

The materials used to make lampshades are quite varied. Translucent paper shades, for example, give off a soft glowing effect. Painted shades are quite interesting. Linen, cotton, and silk, whether pleated, shirred, or stretched are beautiful and rich. Color is another consideration. Dead white isn't attractive, but soft pink gives off a wonderful subtle color that makes everyone and everything glow. For the best results, take the lamp with you when selecting the shade. The simplest design made in the best way with the nicest material is the safest rule of thumb.

Bulbs

If you haven't really shopped for bulbs lately, that is, done nothing more than buy replacements for your sixty- and seventy-five-watt bulbs, check it out! There are all sorts of energy-efficient bulbs that give you more light for your money, save energy, and are good for the environment. Many of these bulbs are designed to give off a warm, soft light and you'll need fewer replacements. Further, for your information, your electric company often gives away pamphlets on energy-efficient lighting, one hundred ways to control your electric bill, and tips for electrical safety at home.

ꝏ Cozy Up for Winter

Once summer is over we tend to concentrate on putting away out-door furniture, cleaning the barbecue grill, and taking a look at what we need to make living indoors more comfortable. When the air begins to feel chilly it's a good time to make your home a cheer-ful, warm, inviting place to enhance the spirit, soothe the soul, and conjure up dreams for the future. But before decorating you may want to get organized by getting rid of things that have outlived their usefulness to make room for new things you might want to buy. Concentrate on a few square inches of space at a time and you'll make inroads toward greeting the onset of fall/winter, and the idea of putting your whole house, or life, in order won't seem so daunting.

Getting Organized

During the summer months you may have neglected closets, drawers, and other storage areas. It's easy to put off small chores like organizing a linen closet, for example, until a rainy day. Make a list of the small and larger things that need attention. As a suggestion, why not begin by cleaning out one kitchen drawer and getting rid of unnecessary clutter. This might mean throwing away old, stained, or unappealing napkins and dish towels. If you don't have time for much else you can revel in opening that one drawer every time you need a "feel good" moment.

Making a "To Do" List

Making "to do" lists can be enormously satisfying. Armchair organizing is a prelude to action. Avoid the gift and toy catalogs. They are intended to provoke anxiety. It isn't time to think about the holidays until your home is ready to accept the decorations and you have a clear surface to wrap gifts and a place to keep the fixings. With this in mind, try to organize things in see-through plastic containers that fit into closets. Label the outsides of the containers.

Making Time for the Things You Enjoy

My daughter Robby is easing into making holiday gifts. She's created a work space in her basement and has the sewing machine set up. Every time she does a load of laundry, she uses that exact time for crafting. By the time the wash is done her allocated crafting time is up. At this rate she figures she can avoid that overwhelming feeling of too little time as the holidays get closer. Whatever the craft, she has a basket for leftover scraps. She gives these to her two little boys to make their own projects while she's working on hers. You might do the same, filling a basket with glue, paper, pieces of wood, stickers, fabric scraps, stars, buttons, and sequins. Organize your crafting material in easy-to-take-out-and-put-away containers like baskets or plastic storage boxes.

Keeping Things in Good Order

If you enjoy setting a pretty table for the holidays, start early and take stock of napkins, tablecloth, silver and brass items. Wash and iron, remove spots, and polish whatever needs attention. Not waiting until the last minute will make you feel terrific. It's also a good time to put away knickknacks you've grown tired of looking at, or those "extra" items that seem to creep into our spaces. It's also a good time to cozy up your rooms with things you may have put away like quilts or a mohair throw.

Home Office

Most of us have a home office area even if it's just a desk in one corner of a room for paying bills and writing letters. Examine how you could make this area look and function better. There are all sorts of good-looking containers, file boxes, desk lamps, and organizers for this purpose. Update what you have. You might like a sleek modern look, or use antique objects for a different feeling. Be creative. For example, an unused silver teapot might be the perfect vase for flowers. I like glass votive candleholders and ceramic plant pots for holding pens and pencils. And I use a silver baby cup to hold paper clips. A brass toast holder from London keeps my notecards and envelopes organized.

Photographs

After a summer of picture-taking you might want to sort through and select the best photos suitable for framing. Take a half day to do this and allocate a shelf, tabletop, or small wall area for your display. Replace old photos with new ones, if you've run out of room.

Books

It's hard to get rid of books. But the old paperbacks could free up space for your more current interest. A bookshelf doesn't have to be used strictly for holding books. Intersperse the area with a small plant, a pretty piece of porcelain, a framed picture to break up the solid mass created by rows of books. Also, books can add interest when piled here and there in a room. I have a small child's chair that I use for books or an occasional plant. I also use a small footstool to hold books.

Making More Room in the Bathroom

Nobody ever feels they have enough room in their bathroom. Even gaining a little bit of extra shelf space can be helpful. Throw away old cosmetics and ratty towels, and replace an old bath mat. How long has it been since you read the labels on medicine in the cabinet or refrigerator? Check the dates and throw away those that have outlived their effectiveness. Make an edited version of a first-aid box to have on hand in a kitchen drawer for quick access. Clean out the medicine cabinet. These little organizing projects won't take long, but will be enormously satisfying.

୫୦ Brighten Up Winter Grayness

Over my desk hangs a group of small framed photographs from one of our trips. The photographs represent typical, carefree summer days filled with sunshine and bicycle baskets holding flowers. Windowsills hold terra-cotta pots filled with pink geraniums, and lace curtains blow in the gentle breeze. I find these pictures comforting to look at in the dead of winter.

I sometimes forget that not everyone lives in a gray and white world in the wintertime. Some people live where it's technicolor all year long. But for the rest of us, here are some suggestions for brightening our homes and actually taking advantage of winter without leaving home.

Flowers

There's nothing like the sight of fresh flowers in the middle of the winter to make a house cheerful. I have small plants with white blossoms and dark green leaves in painted clay pots. They sit on shelves in the kitchen and in a rustic basket on my dining table. They are clean and pure and just the ticket for spots of living things to remind me of spring.

The other day I sat staring at my stair risers. They looked dreadful. Didn't we just paint those a few months ago? I thought. This is a terrific time to take stock of small areas of your house, like windowsills and baseboards, and give them all a touch-up. It will put you way ahead of spring when it arrives and you really would rather be in the garden. Plus, this is one of the cheapest ways to improve the look of your house for practically no effort or money.

Cooking for Later

While it's cold outdoors, use the time to make double batches of dinners that can be put away in the freezer for days when you'd rather do other things. It's fun to experiment with dishes on winter weekends, and just the heat and smells from cooking will add warmth and cheer to your home. You might also use the indoor time to get creative with your cooking so you can set a stylish table with a meal to complement it.

Rearrange Furniture

Arranging furniture is one of my favorite activities. Try a new arrangement that might make a room cozier for winter. Add a colorful wool blanket or warm throw to the back of a sofa or chair. Pile books on the coffee table for a spur-of-the moment read on the sofa, wrapped in that warm mohair throw.

Start a New Project

Get all the materials together, create a place to work, and start a project like a cross-stitch sampler or a needlepoint pillow, or learn to faux paint an old piece of furniture. For the third winter in a row I'm seriously considering slipcovering my two love seats. This winter I might just do it! And that's another thing I plan to do, catch up.

Fabric

Most decorators agree that the fastest and easiest way to completely change the feeling of a room is to use fabric. Even a very simple, inexpensive fabric can soften a space and add warmth. Ever thought of upholstering walls? It adds a luxurious feeling to a room, covers up defects, and helps soundproof. It's a classy way to add style for minimal investment.

Decorator's Touch

Furnishing a new house can be overwhelming. Many people seek help from professionals. How can a design professional help you create a well-designed, beautifully put-together, and comfortable house that doesn't look "done"? First, they give you access to showrooms for products, fabrics, and a whole array of colors and styles, sometimes without leaving home. They can help save you costly mistakes and can offer creative ideas for using what you have or solving existing house problems.

Plans for the Future

Even if you don't go so far as to redecorate, planning to do so can be a lot of fun. Create a wish list and keep a scrapbook of cutouts from magazine pages for the things you'd like to have or the look you'd like to achieve if time and money were no object. Collect swatches of fabrics, paint color chips, and free booklets from home centers.

One-of-a-Kind Touches

ℬ Handmade Makes It Special

Whenever I see something that's beyond my budget I usually try to figure out a way to make it myself. Over the years I've learned how to do all sorts of crafts and today it's easier than ever to learn a particular technique because of all the materials available. The nice thing about either making something for your home, or buying something handcrafted is that it adds character and interest and often personalizes an area. Since I own a store in a resort area where we sell handcrafted items, I know that when people are on vacation they often look for unusual home-decorating accessories. This is something that adds to vacation fun. I collect handmade bowls and try to find them whenever I'm traveling. The collection on a shelf above my kitchen cabinets is a reminder of every place I've been.

Crafting Statistics

The Hobby Industry Association recently announced the following: (1) Within 90 percent of households in the United States at least one family member crafts. (2) The top sources of ideas for crafters are magazines (68 percent), family/friends (56 percent), store displays (49 percent), books (41 percent), and catalogs (40 percent). (3) Almost half of craft/hobby participants subscribe to and/or purchase craft publications. (4) Viewing of craft television programs is increasing as well. More than one third of craft participants reported watching these programs in 1998, versus a quarter in 1997.

This last bit of news isn't very surprising, due to the fact that there are twice as many cable shows with craft, decorating, and hobby-related subjects than there were a year ago. Decorating with handmade items and making things to give as gifts are the most popular motivating factors.

News for Stitchers

Lately I've been looking into new products on the market to make crafting easier. For stitchers who like to do needlework you can now buy a sheet of self-sticking, clear ovals that adhere to the tips of your fingers. They are intended to save your fingers from needle pricks and are more comfortable and less cumbersome than thimbles.

I gave them a try. The good news is they actually stick and are pliable. They're easy to peel off when the job is done. You can put them on as many fingers as you're using (as opposed to switching the thimble from finger to finger as you work). The bad news is they aren't strong enough to protect your finger when you push the end of a needle through the fabric. Therefore I'd rate this product good enough to use for some types of work, such as on the finger holding the underside of the fabric you're stitching, but a thimble is still the best for pushing the needle through the fabric. The product is sold in fabric and notions shops.

Everyone Needs Glue

Glue is something we all use in crafting, especially when making holiday ornaments and decorations, cards, decoupage, and such. After researching glue from companies all over the world, I'm still in favor of Elmer's Glue-All. For some types of crafting it's best slightly diluted as it can be too thick for delicate work, such as creating pressed flower pictures and adhering paper to slick surfaces.

A hot glue gun is indispensible for many projects such as

wreath making or working with shells. It's an inexpensive tool that's worth owning if you do a variety of crafts.

Paint

I always use water-based paint. It dries quickly, it's easy to clean brushes, and there are no toxic fumes. Acrylic paint is the best for stenciling and I use latex paint for furniture projects. Many craft companies sell small bottles of acrylic paints that are good for small projects. There are as many shades of colors as you'd ever want. They cost about $2.95 a bottle and you can buy the exact color needed, premixed. They're perfect if you only need a small amount.

There are new spray latex paints on the market that are smooth, fast-drying, and have a nice sheen. Krylon and Rust-Oleum are two reliable brand names. Rust-Oleum also has a line of decorator brush-on paints that come in small cans for crafting and they are wonderful. Their spray enamels come in a wide range of decorator colors and we've been using them in our studio to paint a variety of containers. When spray-painting, remember to do so in a well-ventilated area, and always wear a mask. The paper masks don't provide enough protection. If you intend to do a lot of spraying, invest in a good mask. They're available in all paint departments.

Popular Craft Projects

Wreaths have always been a popular item and you can add distinction to your front door or indoors with a wreath of dried flowers any time of year. A quilted wall hanging is another nice project, and a great inexpensive substitute for artwork. There are several patchwork patterns, such as Around the World or Log Cabin that lend themselves to a wall hanging in bright or pastel colors, in prints or solids. These patterns are easy to cut and stitch together because they are made up of squares or rectangles.

Computerized Patterns

Hot Product Watch: M&R Enterprises PCStitch allows needle-workers to create counted cross-stich patterns on IBM-compatible PCs. The program allows the user to choose from 390 thread colors, which have corresponding DMC, Anchor, and J&P Coats thread numbers, to create a pattern up to 500 by 500 stitches using up to 64 colors. Printouts can be generated in both color and black and white, with symbols representing colors.

꧂ Sew-Easy

There are many simple sewing projects that anyone can do and that will save you lots of money. By making things yourself you'll be surprised at the satisfaction gained, but more than that you'll be able to have many home furnishing items that are quite costly to buy. Slipcovers, for example are almost as expensive as a new sofa or chair. But the fabric cost is the least of it. Recently I amazed myself when I found a beautiful chair at our local landfill. The frame was intact but the upholstery was missing. However, there was a seat and a down cushion in perfect condition. I followed directions in a book on' upholstery and redid the chair with white linen. It is now residing in my living room!

Sewing to Reduce Stress

While millions of dollars have been spent on health club memberships, meditation classes, and/or therapy in an effort to reduce stress, a new clinical study has found that something as simple and rewarding as sewing may be the perfect antidote.

Commissioned by the American Home Sewing & Craft Association, the study reveals that women who sew, both experienced and novice sewers, showed a significant drop in heart rate and blood pressure when compared to women who participate in other leisure-time activities. Moreover, sewing had the greatest overall positive effect on these stress indicators when compared to other activities.

According to *Sew News* magazine, the majority of their readers sew because they enjoy it and because they find it relaxing. Sewing is soothing, even if you've never done it before. It's a creative and satisfying activity that one can do for long stretches of time, or in starts and stops. Furthermore, it's easy to learn how to do simple projects like making curtains, a tablecloth, a patchwork quilt, or throw pillows.

One of the main reasons people sew is to make home decorating elements. Home sewing plays a very positive role in our society, which is undergoing a dynamic reassessment of values. It transforms couch potato passivity into active involvement, without leaving home. In an age where mass production disempowers, hands-on activities like sewing allow people to regain control over their lives. Once you decide to make some basic accessories, go to a high-end home furnishing store or boutique that sells expensive items and really look at the things made from fabric. Then go to a fabric shop and look through the pattern books. Every pattern maker such as Vogue, Butterick, and McCalls has a home decorating section offering patterns for making coordinated sets from kitchen seat covers to curtains in all styles, to easy slipcovers and pillows. All the materials needed, including a wide variety of trimmings and hardware for curtains and draperies, can be found here as well.

Buying a Sewing Machine

My sewing machine is as important to my well-being as my computer. I think of them both as essential tools for my varied creative output. Prices for sewing machines range from $150 to $3,500 with the average machine costing around $1,000. Today's sewing machine is technologically advanced, eliminating the need to thread needles and trim excess thread. Computer memory has enhanced creativity, allowing for elaborate embroidery designs and monogramming. Buttonhole work can be "saved," then repeated identically. Top-of-the-market machines can scan a design from a magazine or newspaper and produce it, incorporating the sewer's own changes and color choices.

Selecting a sewing machine is similar in many ways to selecting a car. You consider its features, durability, and dependability and expect it to last a number of years with a minimum of care and repair. The number and type of features a sewing machine has will affect the price. Consider the features you select as an investment in the development of your sewing skills. If often used, these features will eventually pay for themselves. Three good ways to ensure the quality of your purchase are: select a known brand, buy from a reputable dealer who offers good service, and ask the opinion of friends who are accomplished sewers. Remember the two big "don'ts." Don't pay for more features than you will use, and don't economize by selecting a machine that will fall short of your expectations in a year. Beware of a "too good to be true" deal. You're also buying the service a reputable dealer offers.

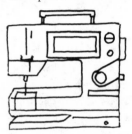

Features to Look For

Certain features are basic necessities, while others are special extras that are nice to have.

Basic Features:

1. Machine starts and stops smoothly and is jam-proof as you sew off the edge of the fabric.
2. Bobbin doesn't vibrate while sewing, and feeds thread evenly.
3. Bobbin is simple to wind and easy to insert into bobbin case.
4. Thread guides are easy to thread.
5. Needle is easy to insert.
6. Variety of easy-to-change attachments.

7. Needle-plate markings to guide seam widths.
8. Accurate reverse stitching.
9. Controllable stitch lengths and widths.
10. Adjustable tension and pressure knobs.
11. Light that illuminates needle area without shadows.
12. Foot pedal is easy and comfortable to operate.
13. Easy to clean.
14. Instruction book you can understand!

Take a Test Drive

New sewers should ask the dealer to take you through a test drive on fabrics of different weights and textures. A precision machine should be able to stitch on a variety of fabric types with equal ease. Look for even stitches with good tension control. If the tension is correct, the stitches will look the same on both the top and bottom of the fabric without puckers.

A Reminder for Experienced Sewers

If you are one of the millions of people who already owns a sewing machine, but haven't stitched for ages, take advantage of a rainy day. Clean and oil up your machine and take a trip through the fabric shops. It's like visiting a spring garden in full bloom and will almost make you forget what's going on outside.

✃ Distressed Furniture

Refinishing old furniture is one way to save money and furnish a room with an interesting item. There are many ways to do this. Distressed furniture has become quite popular and looks especially good in a country setting. However, I've seen many such pieces in contemporary environments, often lending charm to the rest of the furnishings. If you find a piece of furniture with good lines but the finish isn't perfect, you might consider a crackle finish to make it look even older but better-looking than it is.

Crackle Finish

This is a glazed finish that looks as though the painted surface is cracked overall. The appearance is like that of a cracked eggshell. Crackle glaze was invented in France in the eighteenth century. It was inspired by the lacquer finish of imported Oriental ceramics and Japanese Raku pottery. Today it is used by faux finishers to add faded character to a painted piece of furniture, moldings, picture and mirror frames.

How to Do It

For small projects that require quick crafting, Plaid Enterprises makes a product called "crackle paint" and it's available in most craft stores. However, to make the real thing, especially if you're planning to paint furniture, the process involves applying two interacting varnishes over each other. Ready-made crackle lacquer is sold in art stores as a pack of two varnishes and you will also need transparent oil glaze, raw umber oil paint (comes in small tubes), and cheesecloth. Here's how it's done:

1. Start with a painted piece in a color of your choice. It can be painted with any base such as latex or oil enamel. The piece should be cleaned of dirt by first sanding lightly.
2. Apply the oil-based varnish in a smooth, thin layer. Let the varnish dry until slightly tacky.
3. Brush on a coat of water-based varnish, covering the entire surface completely. Leave to dry for about an hour. Cracks will appear.
4. To accentuate the cracks and give the piece an antiqued look, mix a small amount of raw umber with a tablespoonful of transparent oil glaze. Use the cloth to rub the mixture all over the surface.
5. Rub away the excess without removing it from the cracks.

Leave this to dry for several days. You can then apply a coat of oil-based varnish if you want or simply wipe it all over with a damp sponge, leaving traces of color in the cracks.

6. If you want to use a specific color you can either paint the background in that color or use the color rather than raw umber to give the cracks a brighter look.

Accessories That Do the Trick

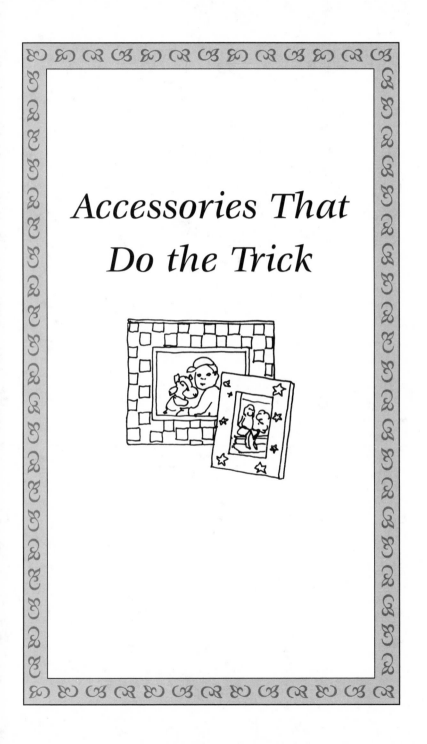

❧ Warm Fuzzies: Using the Things You Love

When moving to a new home the question is always what to keep and what to get rid of. Moving into a first home presents other problems. You may wonder how you'll ever furnish all the rooms. My next-door neighbors just sold their house. The yard sale advertised, "Just sold our house. Everything must go." Starting over with bare rooms can be a daunting challenge, scary or exciting. There are many ways to make a comfortable transition from bare to fully furnished.

Make Room for the Old

Once their children were grown, a couple sold their family home and moved into a smaller one. They knew exactly which pieces of furniture had to go with them and kept this in mind when looking for a new house. Theirs was an accumulation of things they had acquired carefully and over many years. Many of their furnishings are associated with a lifetime of memories. In a new home, familiar things are comforting and make the transition to the new space more comfortable.

Starting from Scratch

If you're moving into your first home and have limited funds, don't turn down anything your relatives may offer unless you really hate it. Even if your taste is modern, you'll find that a few homey items like your grandmother's rocking chair, an old quilt, or a faded love seat can be positively charming in a contemporary setting. Remember, too, that something with good lines but a bad finish, such as a really scratched or stained bureau, can be stripped and refinished for pennies and a few hours of your time. In today's market this can amount to a substantial savings and your new piece will probably be worth a great deal more than anything you might buy. Old pieces of furniture were often made better as well.

Making Your Own Comfort

Even if you don't have old and wonderful things with which to surround yourself, you can create a warm environment with things you find and love. My daughter-in-law is in love with all things from the Victorian era. They live in an old farmhouse and she spends a great deal of time going to auctions, yard sales, and the antique market. Her house is filled with wonderful old pieces that she's acquired piece by piece as she could afford them. Everything in the house looks like it might have been inherited, creating a warm and comfortable feeling. Sometimes a few antiques from a past era that you're attracted to will add to the charm of your new environment. You don't have to adhere strictly to one style once you start on this path. Mixing styles is far more interesting.

A Little Goes a Long Way

Decorators often get rid of the old when the urge for change takes a grip. When a well-known decorator I know sold his house in town, he simply put a lot of his furniture out on his front lawn for anyone to take. "I wanted the new house to dictate the furnishings, rather than the other way around," he told me.

For most of us, it's financially impractical to get rid of everything and start over. Furniture is expensive. For young people starting out, it's hard enough to acquire a home, let alone furnish it. If this is your situation, work around what you have. Slipcover an old sofa in new, up-to-date fabric, for example. If this is beyond your ability, camouflage it with lots of fresh new throw pillows in an array of smashing fabrics. Be daring with color because you can always change the look next season by simply changing the pillows.

Think Like a Decorator

Designing for clients isn't always as satisfying as doing one's own home. However, most decorators will tell you their homes are never done. Anyone in a creative business is forever involved in the pursuit of perfecting their lifestyle and environment as an extended means of creative expression. This interest is not limited to those with a creative bent, however.

Most people with busy lives have no time for decorating and yet we want our homes to be comfortable and good looking. The answer is simple. Decorate slowly. If you can conceive of living with a dining table and no chairs, until you find the ones that are absolutely right for you, then don't feel guilty about using folding metal chairs in the meantime. Just buy inexpensive slipcovers for the chairs (they're available through discount stores and mail-order catalogs) and remember that you don't have an empty room, but rather that you're in the process of decorating—for however long it takes.

Temporarily Furnished

If your living room looks too uninviting, do a little cosmetic surgery. Pull whatever furniture you have away from the walls and create a cozy and intimate seating area. If you have a coffee table or end table but nothing to go on it, fill it with books, inexpensively framed photographs, a souvenir from your travels, and anything else you have that you enjoy looking at. A photo album filled with favorite family photos is perfect. It doesn't take too many things to create a lived-in, personal space.

When you use an inappropriate piece of furniture in place of what will eventually be there, it gives you an approximation of the look you want. You can always camouflage it with a few interesting objects like a pretty bowl filled with potpourri, a glass animal, and a vase.

More Tricks of the Trade

To make a room feel furnished, fill large crocks with tall branches of fronds, leaves, or marsh grasses. Fill oversize vases with branches of evergreens and place them on the floor next to a sofa. A small table covered with a tapestry cloth can serve as a temporary end table, again with an interesting piece of pottery on top. Low lamps would be the next obvious purchase for making the room seem cozy.

What to Do with Bare Walls

If you don't have any artwork, hang a small quilted wall hanging for instant warmth. If you're lucky enough to own an old quilt that's beyond repair, consider cutting out a good section and having it framed. This might be just what the room needs to create a homey feeling. Photographs lend another familiar touch. It's easy to find inexpensive frames that look every bit as good as expensive ones. If you have a fireplace, the mantel is a great place to display framed family photographs.

Another trick is to matte and frame greeting cards, pages from an illustrated book, or pages from a botanical calendar.

ℰℴ Collections

Americans love to shop. Our homes are testament to our acquisitions, and collecting is a passion shared by many. What people collect is a subject that never ceases to be fascinating. You can find information about almost anything that attracts you. The pursuit of a collectible is as much fun as the acquisition itself and, if one isn't careful, can lead to obsessive behavior. Who among us doesn't know someone crazy for something?

What to Collect

A few collectibles continue to hold a fascination. They may have interesting historic backgrounds, they may be especially well designed, or they may continue to increase in monetary value because of their rarity. For whatever reason, there is never a dirth of collectibles or people who want to collect them. Here are a few interesting items that are affordable and add a special touch to a room.

Cloisonné

This is enamelwork that is often described as a rather exuberant art form. It originated during the early years of the Ming dynasty and was most often used for small boxes, plates, bowls, flower vases, and lady's compacts. It has never really been taken seriously because it's often considered rather gaudy. Originally intended to imitate precious stones, it has thrived for over six hundred years.

In the 1800s the Palace of Fountainebleau in France featured a room filled with cloisonné. It appeared again when the Victoria and Albert Museum opened in 1889. In Chinese, the term *cloisoné* means "the blue of the Ching-T'ai," named after an early Ming dynasty monarch.

Antique Duck Decoys

Most collectible duck decoys were made between 1880 and 1939 and have become quite popular. Because of this they are extremely hard to find, especially in their original state. Often reheaded or repainted, or even recently carved and made to look old, it is hard to tell what is an antique and what isn't. Check carefully. Because the neck is the weakest point, the heads of antique decoys often break off and need to be repaired. You can usually tell if a new head or an old one has been glued to the body.

Creamware

Creamware is giving majolica, faience, and delft a good run for the money. Some consider this chic pottery more valuable. Personally, I love the cream-colored earthenware. The color is so subtly this side of white, and the extraordinary workmanship can still be appreciated today. I love the soft glow and smooth feel of the creamy brilliant glaze. When set on a table these pieces are simply elegant under candlelight.

Creamware came into vogue between 1760 and 1790 and spread throughout Europe. In this country, a Wedgwood potter named John Bartram began making it in 1770. Teapots, coffeepots, and pitchers were made on a potter's wheel, while plates, handles, tableware, and elaborate decorations were press-molded. Notable openwork fruit baskets and stands were intricately produced by Josiah Wedgwood, who created a better glaze that was immune to crazing and pitting, resulting in exceptionally beautiful and pure creamware.

When looking for creamware don't be put off if a piece isn't marked. Most of these pieces don't have markings on them. However, the marks of a few early makers are Herculaneum Pottery, Davenport, Wedgwood, Spode, Leeds, Neale & Co., and Turner. Check for repairs, especially on handles and edges. If a piece seems excessively thick, it was probably made in the late 1800s, a century after the height of the creamware period. If you have such pieces, it is best not to put them in the dishwasher.

Fiestaware

Another pottery of an entirely different sort, Fiestaware is making a comeback. This dinnerware, rather heavy, and distinguishable because of its pastel and gaudy colors, was designed in 1936. Its art deco styling, featuring concentric circles and eleven brilliantly colored glazes was produced through 1969. When it was reintroduced in 1986 in new colors, it became popular all over again. Its jaunty style and serviceable practicality make it a favorite for everyday use, especially in the form of coffee mugs and breakfast bowls.

℘ Silverware

I've always been attracted to silverware and china that was once used on elegant ocean liners and in fine dining cars on trains. Or those used for setting tables in better hotels. Probably part of a bygone era, institutional silverware from public eating places is collected for many reasons. Nostalgia for more refined times is one. Quality is another part of their appeal, as is their simple, traditional design.

How It Was Made

According to a source at Reed and Barton, Corp., commercial flatware, the kind found in better hotels, was made by electroplating a heavy coat of pure silver on a white nickel silver base. This produced flatware that could withstand constant use without losing its shine or shape. The large-size sturdy silverware is great for everyday use and perfect for setting an interesting table, which, in my opinion, deems it worthy of owning.

While the silver-plating process was invented in England in 1742, American silversmiths perfected the technique in the 1840s. In the mid–nineteenth century silver-plated flatware became an excellent step up from inexpensive tin and was not as expensive as silverware. The upwardly mobile middle class embraced it with enthusiasm. The railroad dining cars and grand hotels exposed people to a wonderful variety of specially made pieces that were designed in the style of the times.

Different Styles

Items like this are part of our American culture. You might, for example, be attracted to the art deco style of furnishing. It's possible to find silverware manufactured during the 1920s through the early 1930s to complement your taste. Collecting can get pretty specific, narrowing in on a certain period, style, color (in the case of chinaware or ceramics), or it can be quite general. Often, the longer a collector collects, the more specific and refined the collection becomes.

Sources for Old Silverware

Silverware such as this is not all that hard to find. It crops up routinely at flea markets, yard sales, thrift shops, and antique stores. These pieces are relatively inexpensive, averaging between $3 and $10, depending on the design or where it's from. I once found a set of silver-plated forks in an antique shop in Arizona. I was attracted to their hefty size and the deep engraved symbol on each handle. They are rugged and good-looking and we use them all the time. Many shops now carry reproductions of early silverware that's just as good looking as the real thing.

It Doesn't Have to Match

Those who collect silverware say it doesn't have to match. It's wonderful if you come upon a complete set from one source, as a gentleman I met did at the marketplace in Provence. However, mixing and matching can make your table all the more interesting, as will other assorted items like creamers, pitchers, and teapots or coffeepots. While I don't serve tea or coffee from the art deco coffeepot and teapot I inherited from my grandmother, I use both these servers for holding flowers. The pitcher and creamer have become lovely desk accessories for holding pens and pencils as well as bunches of summer roses. There is something quite lovely about a bouquet of roses in an elaborately etched silver teapot.

A Lucky Find

If you haven't given vintage silverware a thought, you might do so if you happen to stumble on a carton of odds and ends at a rummage sale. Don't be too quick to pass it by. Rummage a bit. You might find the beginning of a collection. If you're lucky enough to find something rare, it could be the start of a meaningful love affair.

ℬ Unusual Accessories

Whenever I need a finishing touch on a coffee table, for a small wall area, or to be used as a centerpiece I look for something unusual that doesn't cost a lot. Sometimes it's fun to imagine what small luxury you'd like to receive as a gift and then buy it for yourself.

Marine Theme

Marine-related objects are of interest to many collectors and while some are quite expensive, there is always something for everyone's pocketbook. For example, someone who enjoys fishing as a pastime might like to display colorful fishing lures. I've seen beautifully painted metal and wooden fish decorating the walls of a family room. Painted buoys are often better suited to hanging on the wall than for use on a boat. Ship models come in different sizes, quality, and prices and can look terrific over a mantel, in a bookshelf, or on top of an armoire, for example. For those interested in marine artifacts you might look for seafaring paintings, beautifully framed maps, and fish prints, a brass telescope, sailor's valentines, and scrimshaw.

Boxes of All Sorts

Lots of people collect boxes, both old and new, and they're easy to find in antique shops, flea markets, and thrift shops. Boxes can be both good-looking and practical. I have an old thread box with a company name stenciled on the front. Inside I display spools of silk thread I found at a yard sale. Stacks of Shaker boxes and old spice boxes are among others I've seen in Early American homes.

Handcrafts

Small carved or sculpted items such as shore birds, duck decoys, blown-glass pitchers, pottery, paperweights, and hand-painted candlesticks are just a few items that can be found in craft stores in every price range. It's fun to find something handmade that might become the beginning of a collection.

Photo Albums

Creating an interesting photo album is always fun. Perhaps you can find an exceptionally good-looking album that would be perfect to leave out on a coffee table. This is always a tempting diversion for guests and family members. And if you have a favorite photograph, have it enlarged and professionally framed for hanging.

Shells

While on vacation in Florida, I purchased a bagful of exotic shells. In a gift shop, I found the perfect oval bowl in a wonderful pale lavender color. The white and yellow shells fill the bowl and make a delightful accent on a table in my entryway. (Of course, you don't have to *purchase* sea shells—you can pick them up where they wash up along the shore, too.)

Silver Objects

There are all sorts of small and interesting silver objects, from sterling snuff boxes to silver plated bottle stoppers. A friend of mine has the most interesting silver charm bracelets, which she displays on a shelf.

Bottles

Old bottles can be quite interesting, and they are inexpensive. I line them on a shelf across my kitchen window and fill each with buds of flowers. Antique perfume bottles make an interesting display on a bathroom shelf.

Decorating for Special Occasions

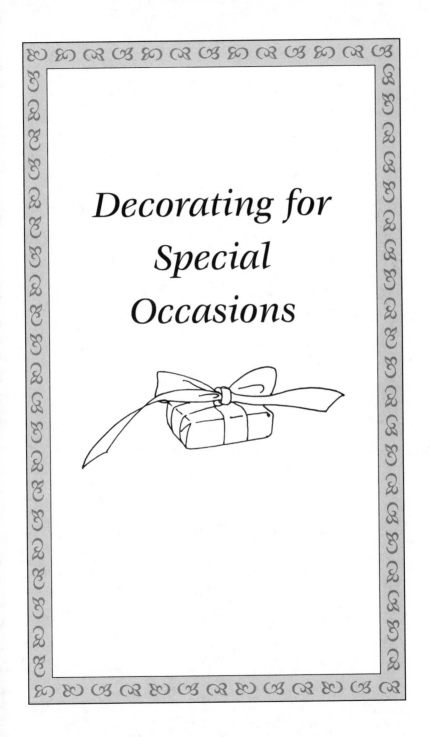

ℰℴ Decorations for a Kid's Party

If you enjoy decorating for a party, don't stop with the adults. One of the most successful events I attended this year took place at the elegant home of friends and was given in honor of their visiting grandchild's fourth birthday.

The invited guests were under six years old and they were allowed to bring their parents. Not a detail was overlooked in the decorations, food and its presentation, entertainment, prizes, and the cake. For two busy people, my friends seamlessly and beautifully blended a party for both the children and their parents. The theme of the party was trains, and it was enjoyed by boys and girls alike. This should give you ideas for your next to-do, whether for children or adults.

A Table Set for a Child

The dining table was laden with an elegant spread for the parents. But, never losing sight of the fact that this was a kiddie party, the centerpiece was a large Tonka truck filled with plump ripe peaches.

A side table held the children's buffet, which consisted of baby carrots, chicken fingers, and tiny potato cups, each decorated with a flag from a different country. Two children's tables were set on the screened-in porch. But there wasn't a paper plate in sight. Children were treated with the party respect one would extend to adults.

Each child's dinner was beautifully arranged on blue scalloped china plates. And the children behaved the way they were treated.

Each table held a centerpiece made by filling a large terra-cotta pot with ripe cherries, and at each child's place there was a brightly colored plastic train filled with take-home gifts. Large colorful buckets of ice held bottles of soda on a side table. No paper napkins for this party. Oversize bandannas in bright party colors were spread across pint-sized laps or tied, bib-style around little necks. Carrying out the theme, the birthday cake was made in the shape of a train.

Entertainment

Kids love a piñata and it was easy to string one from a ceiling where there was plenty of room all around for the children to take turns at whacks. As each child left, they were given a colorful bag of candy and a train whistle. "That was the best party I ever went to," Sara, age five, remarked as we left laden with goodies.

ℰ Great Bridal Shower Decorations

It's wedding time and with it comes an array of parties, including the bridal shower. This ritual party might be given by the maid of honor, a close relative of the bride, or several good friends. Until very recently this was a "girls only" affair. However, just as the traditional newspaper engagement announcement photo featuring the bride-to-be sans groom has given way to a more modern version of the couple pictured together, so has the traditional shower yielded to a mixed crowd.

Showers with a Theme

The purpose of a shower is still to bestow upon the bride-to-be the tangible necessities of married life that don't qualify as bona fide wedding gifts. These parties often have themes such as "a kitchen shower" or an "intimate shower," where the gifts might be dish towels or lace undies. Some parties carry the theme through the decorations and food and even the entertainment.

Many year ago, while working on a book called *Making It Personal*, we designed what we called a "keepsake tablecloth" for a shower. It was such a nice idea and I received many letters from people telling me of their success with the project. It's still quite lovely and perhaps something you and your friends might enjoy doing for an upcoming bride. The theme might be "Entertaining," with guests asked to bring gifts intended to enhance the idea that entertaining in style is part of the joys of married life.

How to Make a Keepsake Tablecloth

The Keepsake Tablecloth begins with a plain linen cloth. Purchase one in a pretty, solid color, no pattern. The idea is to create a petal design in the center of the cloth with the number of petals equal to the number of guests. The flower is embroidered in the center and each guest's signature is embroidered on each petal. There are many personalizing ser-

vices that do custom embroidery such as this; it just takes a bit of planning. Or, if one of the guests does needlework, this is an easy hand-embroidered project to do with simple embroidery stitches such as the chain, back, or feather stitches.

Directions:

1. Use the petal design provided on page 199 and have it enlarged at a copy center to the full length of an 11 × 17-inch paper. Trace one petal and make a copy for each guest. Send it with the invitation along with a stamped envelope. Ask each guest to sign his or her name within the petal outline and return it to you.

2. Using tracing paper and a soft pencil, trace the outline of each enlarged petal to create the flower.

3. Trace the signatures of each guest in position within each petal on the paper.

4. Turn the tracing paper over and go over each line of the signature and petals of the flower with a soft pencil.

5. Turn the tracing right side up, and tape it to the center of the tablecloth.

6. Transfer the designs by burnishing each line carefully with the closed end of a marker or similar object. Lift a corner of the tracing paper, and carefully check to be sure the transfer is taking to the cloth before you remove it. If the pattern appears light, apply more pressure over the tracing lines.

7. At this point the outlines are ready to be embroidered. You might like to vary the embroidery on the signatures by using the stem stitch or back stitch for each one, and a chain stitch for the petals. If you like the idea of personalizing gifts, consider buying lovely, oversize damask or linen napkins, and have a monogram embroidered in one corner of each.

Centerpiece with a Theme

Continuing the theme of entertaining, consider a centerpiece comprised of a large basket filled with the wonderful accessories one might need for a well-dressed table. The gifts could be anything from a box of pure white candles in varying sizes, to totally unnecessary but exceedingly wonderful luxuries such as a silver candle snuffer. You might ask every guest to bring a family recipe on a file card to include in a recipe box for the newlyweds. Gifts might run the gamut from a favorite cookbook to antique cocktail napkins.

Make Your Own Centerpiece

Many high-priced boutiques and garden shops sell beautiful items that can be used to hold plants or cut flowers. Some are made of lacy wrought iron and, while quite beautiful, also come with a high price tag. It's not too difficult to simulate the look if you don't mind spending an hour of your time. Begin with a piece of chicken wire approximately twelve to fourteen inches square. Place it on newsprint and spray-paint it white. Leave to dry, then turn it over and paint the other side. When it is completely dry, mold the wire around a bowl or pot in the desired size. Then remove the bowl and line the wire mold with moss before inserting a florist's vase of delicate white flowers. You might also weave satin ribbon in and out of the wire and insert flower buds here and there to dress it up further. Placed on a lacy tea cloth over the tablecloth this would be perfect for an afternoon party.

More Theme Ideas

Theme parties can be a lot of fun, especially if you suggest that each guest bring something "unusual," "sentimental," "nostalgic," "lacy," or more specifically it might be "kitchen gadgets," "something blue," "anything sexy," or "made of glass." If all your guests have known one another since childhood, the field of creative theme ideas is limitless. Pick anything from your shared childhood and create a party around that idea. Don't forget to dig up old baby pictures or pictures taken at important milestones. Create a photo album that everyone will enjoy. While it's the bride's party, it should be fun for all.

Eggs-actly to Match

Create a color scheme for your bridal shower and make a centerpiece to match. Hard-boil a dozen eggs and dye them as you would for Easter in a variety of pastel colors. Mix food coloring with a teaspoon of vinegar and leave some eggs in the dye bath longer than others to create different shades of color. Fill a basket with the eggs and intersperse with flowers, baby's breath, and lacy greens.

Refreshments

When planning the refreshments, consider where and when you'll be having the party. For example, if you're short on space, a box lunch might be fun. Rather than setting a table for a sit-down meal, one party giver packed separate lunches in little boxes and handed them to each of the guests at the appropriate time. Make the boxes look like little gifts with pretty organdy ribbons around each and a name tag as well. A cake and champagne party might be preferable to a luncheon or dinner. Or, create a party around desserts and have a grand array of all sorts of delectables.

Planning Is Key

The nicest thing about a shower party is there are no rules. It can be whatever appeals to you. However, the more preplanning you do the better. Just be sure it's festive and pretty so everyone, not just the guest of honor, feels honored. And if the guest list is getting out of hand, share the burden. It's not unusual for the bridesmaids to throw the shower jointly. However, one person should take the lead, make lists, and in general be the committee leader to keep everyone on track. The more organized you are beforehand, the more at ease and comfortable everyone will be when it all comes together.

ɛↄ Decorating for the Fourth of July

When celebrating the grand ole Fourth we're always drawn to a theme of stars and stripes. It's a good excuse to dress up our homes in a color and design scheme we might not use at any other time of year. It's fun to set a table for a July Fourth celebration, because you don't have to rack your brain for a creative idea. The color scheme has already been established and it's easy to do. It's even permissible to use disposable items.

Unusual Tablecover

Don't be afraid to use a quilt as a tablecover. Quilts were meant to be used and washed over and over again. They just get softer and better-looking with use.

You can find inexpensive new quilts in all sizes and colors. You might find one in a red, white, and blue theme for this holiday. Mine is made of homespun fabric, which is heavier than other cotton material. The colors are navy, cranberry, and white plaids. So while it carries the red, white, and blue theme, the colors are not quite so bright. After the holiday it makes a perfect twin bed cover. If you don't have a quilt, consider covering your table with a printed fabric in these colors.

Sheets Are Fabulous for Tablecovers

Fieldcrest Cannon offers a sheet design of red and white bold stripes that would make a perfect tablecloth. After your party, wash it and use it on your bed with a soft white cotton blanket. For the table fill a basket with delicate blue lobelia plants and use it as a centerpiece on the red-and-white-striped sheet/tablecloth. The periwinkle color of the flowers surrounded by the bright green lacy stems and leaves is a sensational look. I have a basket filled with this plant on my blue shop door and everyone comments on how beautiful it is. It's a common, inexpensive plant available in most garden centers.

A Do-It-Yourself Tablecloth

You can have a sensational look for your tablecloth without spending any money. Buy a piece of plain blue fabric large enough to cover your table and hang down a few inches all around. You might have to stitch two pieces together to get the width you need, which is easy enough. Or, an inexpensive polyester sheet should do the trick. Then cover it with white stars. Here's how to do it: Use waxed stencil paper and a craft knife to cut a few star shapes in different sizes. Then use masking tape to secure the stencil on the fabric and apply white acrylic paint with a stencil brush to the cutout area. Pick up the stencil and reposition it anywhere on the fabric. Continue to stencil stars in a random pattern all over the background.

Napkins Are Easy to Make

I always use cloth napkins, even for a picnic at the beach, and I usually make my own. It's so easy, and when you do it yourself you can make them extra large. Red plaid or blue-and-white-checked ones are perfect for the Fourth. It's easy to stitch up a bunch of napkins in different fabrics using the red, white, and blue theme. For solid blue napkins, consider one stenciled star on one corner (if you're already stenciling the tablecloth).

Easier Than Homemade

One of the easiest and most practical ways to set a holiday table outdoors is to use blue-and-white-checked linen dish towels as placemats. Then tie red-and-white-plaid linen dish towels with a knot in the center to use for your napkins. A friend of mine once used red, white, and blue washcloths for her barbecue napkins. They looked great, and after dinner she simply threw them into the washing machine.

A Jaunty Centerpiece

White enamel cooking pots with red- or blue-painted rims are popular yard sale items. You may already have some. If not try to find a large white enamel lobster pot with a red rim and fill it with red geraniums. If you can't find that, use a basket or large white bowl.

Inexpensive Plant Holder

For a quick and cheap plant holder spray-paint a large, white, paper paint bucket in red, white, or blue. These can be found in the paint section of your home center for under a dollar. And if you feel particularly creative, why not sponge-paint a contrasting color over the painted background? I demonstrated sponge painting on one of my taped shows for Lifetime and taught the host how to do it right on the spot. When he asked what happens if you make a mistake, my answer was simple: "You can't." This is the most foolproof faux-painting technique you can do.

Give New Life to Ordinary Household Items

Look around the house for interesting containers to fill with red, white, or blue flowers. It could be a pitcher, a box lined with a waterproof container, a tin, or a pretty ceramic bowl. I often fill a plain glass mason jar with flowers from the garden, and am amazed at how charming it looks.

Decorating with Colorful Food

For a simple but elegant decoration, fill a basket with shiny red apples or a plain bowl with ripe red strawberries dotted with blueberries, and set into your basket. If it's last minute, look around your house for anything red, white, and blue and use it to make a display. It might be a blue bowl, a child's small red car or wagon, and a pot of white impatiens. No white flowers? Fill a blue or red bowl with white eggs.

A Seashore Theme

Many of us have a collection of shells from a vacation at the beach. Use them to set a summertime table. Pile them into a basket and use in the center of your picnic table. Add a couple of votive candles set into large clamshells. Or simply scatter shells around a single potted geranium on the table.

All Tied Up

If you're having friends or family over for a buffet meal, wrap the silverware in each napkin and tie with three strands of red, white, and blue fabric. Insert a tiny party flag and a few more into the dirt of a plant and you don't have to do much more. It's amazing how the bright color combination makes everything immediately festive.

All-American Theme

When buying items for my shop I found some small baskets, just large enough to hold napkins, a plant, or plastic eating utensils for a cookout. They are stenciled with the American flag motif and I bought them because people visiting Nantucket from other countries seem to like anything with an American theme. However, so do we, I discovered, when they were quickly gobbled up by islanders. I guess I'll have to start stenciling baskets, which could be a lot of fun. So, if you do stencil that holiday tablecloth, you may fall in love with the white stars on blue and add them to a basket, napkins, even the backs of chair rungs. It's a bold, graphic design that can be in style all year long. Have a bang-up Fourth of July!

Holiday Decorating Made Easy

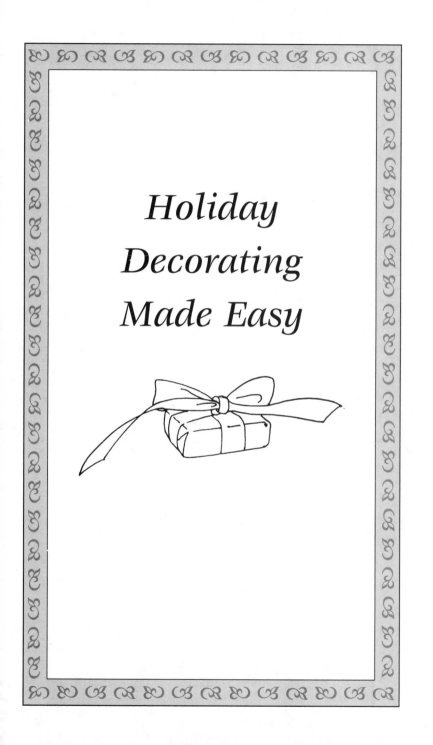

๕ Thanksgiving Table

The week before Thanksgiving is a good time to think about setting the table and what you'll need for making it look extra special. For example, take a walk and gather natural materials for a centerpiece. At the same time, you can plan to use these items for a Christmas wreath. Leaves and pinecones are easy to find or, if you live in a city, visit your local garden center.

Great-Looking Centerpieces

Here are some suggestions for a Thanksgiving centerpiece from the simple to the lavish, depending on how much time you want to devote to it.

1. On a polished wooden table, fill a wooden bowl, basket, large platter, or tray with a variety of polished apples and pears surrounded by nuts, figs, dates, pineapple, and grapes. Use wooden candleholders with earth-colored candles.

2. Cover your table with a pretty tablecloth and use any interesting country container, a crock, a rustic basket, or an antique tin to hold dried flowers in the colors found in the tablecloth. Surround with votive candle holders.

3. Arrange a variety of leaves in the center of the table and top with brightly varnished gourds in different sizes and shapes. Scoop out a hole in the tops of tiny pumpkins or squash to hold candles at different heights.

4. For a formal table setting, spray artificial fruit with gold paint and arrange in a glass bowl. Use a white linen tablecloth, napkins, and white candles in glass candleholders. Or, if you are in a crafting mood, spray-paint small terra-cotta pots with the gold to hold fat white candles.

5. For an interesting tablecloth, use a few yards of heavy unbleached muslin. Prewash it and don't iron it. The fabric will have the nice soft crinkly look often found in old quilts. Fill an interesting container with oranges, grapefruit, lemons, and limes and insert sprigs of pine, holly branches, or tied bundles of cinnamon sticks between the fruit.

6. Make a pinecone basket. All you need is a good-size basket, a bunch of pinecones, and a hot glue gun. Arrange the pinecones in rows around the basket and glue in position so the entire outside of the basket is covered with the pinecones. Fill the basket with fresh sprigs of fir or pine branches, arrange polished red apples on top, and scatter a few cranberries over the greens. Tie the handle with a wide, French wired ribbon in a deep hunter green or cranberry color with gold edges.

7. Fresh cranberries make a wonderful centerpiece. Fill a pretty bowl (preferably white or red and white) with cranberries. Set the bowl on a paper doily or lace place mat in the center of the table. Surround the bowl with evergreens and put tapered candles in the cranberry bowl.

8. A nice table dressing is an arrangement of three pots of fresh herbs down the center of a country table. Use crisp white napkins tied with green ribbon and tuck a sprig of evergreen under each. Use white plates and place a white votive candle at each place setting.

9. Paperwhite bulbs in a low terra-cotta pot make an elegant and simple centerpiece and will last most of the winter.

10. For another white theme (always my favorite) fill a glass vase or large white pitcher with French tulips (all white if available), or the next best, pale pink. Or, insert three or four stems of freesia in a stem holder placed in the center of a large white bowl.

A Special Celebration

This year I'm going to do something different. Because our family always gathers from hither and yon for this holiday and everyone stays in their respective homes for Christmas, I'm going to combine my Thanksgiving and Christmas celebration with a festive table.

If many of you are in the same situation, where you see your family now and not later, perhaps you'll think about doing the same thing. It's always nice to set a table with family heirlooms if you have them. I also like to take out everything good: silver, chinaware, glass goblets—even if half the guest list is under five years old.

Improvising a Table

If your table isn't large enough to seat everyone, it's easy to extend it with a four- by eight-foot piece of plywood placed on top of the existing table. Then cover the board with a thin piece of cotton quilt batting stapled to the underside. This will pad the table and soften the edges. Felt or flannel would work just as well. The next trick is to find a tablecloth large enough to cover the board. A plain white sheet works just fine as an undercloth over which you might put your great-grandmother's crocheted tablecloth, an old quilt, or a few yards of fabric. If you have a lovely old tablecloth packed away, use it. Don't worry about food or wine stains. Anything can be removed. (Quick trick: If wine is spilled on the cloth, immediately pour salt on the spot. After dinner place it over an upside-down colander and pour boiling water through the cloth from an arm's length height. Run through the washing machine on delicate.)

Winter White

Create a table where everything is white, off white, silver, and gold. Napkins should be crisp white damask tied with gold ribbons. For a festive family gathering such as this, use family photographs for place cards. Insert each picture into a pinecone.

Surprise Centerpiece

Our family is made up equally of adults and children and I rather dislike the idea of a "children's table." If you have small children at your table, create a surprise centerpiece by filling a large country grain scoop, a wooden or glass bowl, or a champagne bucket with small gifts wrapped in silver and gold shiny paper. Intersperse with small gold and silver tree balls, white freesia, and tulips with a few sprigs of evergreens.

Attach one end of a ribbon strip to each gift and lead the other end of the ribbon to each child's place. Sprinkle the table with a variety of nuts and "fairy dust," which is nothing more than silver and gold sequins. Add lots of white candles of different heights in different size holders. Individual white votive candles can grace each place setting.

Begin with White Dishes

Start with white dishes and you can always create a stylish table. It's easy to find pure white or very light cream-colored dishes that are inexpensive. They will always look good on any table and you can use them with mismatched serving dishes, glasses, or whatever. Inexpensive plain white dishes are easily replaced when one is broken or chipped. An all-white table with black napkins and candles in white candle holders is quite dramatic.

Silver and Glass

I prefer serving dishes that are white, silver, or glass. If you're lucky enough to have a family heirloom of ornate silver, or brass candleholders, use them often. If you don't have them, keep your antennae up for these items at yard sales or antique and seconds shops because they make any table setting more elegant. I love the ones I inherited from my grandmother and I really don't worry about the fact that I rarely have time to polish them. If it's important to you, you've probably taken care of this task by now. It matters not to me!

Putting on the Glitz

If all your chairs are mismatched, or you're still using folding metal chairs in the dining room, transform them instantly with those wonderful white or gold chair slipcovers you find in the catalogs. If this isn't in the budget, or it's too late, tie pretty bows made from six-inch-wide golden ribbon to each chair. (How did we live without those French wired ribbons?)

Traditional Is Still In

If my table scheme doesn't appeal to you and tradition is what you're after, here are a few ideas culled from my decorating sources.

1. Cover the center of the table with a bed of bay leaves. Arrange pinecones, clove-studded oranges, lemons, and limes on top. Tie bundles of cinnamon sticks with gold ribbon and place here and there.

2. Fill a large wooden salad bowl with fruit and nuts, and insert sprigs of rosemary.

3. Pears make a nice centerpiece. Arrange them on a bed of moss, ivy, or wood chips.

4. A natural wreath of pinecones and seed pods is the perfect centerpiece. Place a bowl in the center of the wreath and fill with a flower arrangement.

5. Make a table decoration using a dampened ring of florist's foam. Cover the ring by inserting lengths of boxwood, then add white tapers evenly spaced around. Fill the center with a bowl of cranberries, and insert sprigs of greens. This centerpiece will last through Christmas if you put it on a tray and keep it damp. Add colorful ribbon bows to the base of each candle for the holidays.

6. An all-white-and-green theme is refreshingly elegant. A simple flower arrangement of white tulips or roses loosely arranged in a white

bowl or clear glass vase is lovely. Set the table with a white linen cloth and use deep green napkins. If you only have white, tie the napkins with green ribbons and insert a sprig of fresh-smelling herbs.

7. Three miniature topiary trees, terra-cotta pots of herbs, decorative flowerpots, spray-painted gold paper paint buckets are all suggestions for centerpieces.

Not Bound by Tradition

If it's really the last minute and you don't want to fuss, mix and match everything you have for a colorful melange. Don't be bound by tradition. Use unusual containers and items to set a creative table. For example, fill a basket with balls of yarn in fall colors, scoop out holes in the tops of fruit for candleholders, fill a punch bowl with twinkling Christmas tree lights, float flower heads in a silver bowl filled with water, or use a champagne bucket as a vase.

A Meaningful Affair

Since we usually gather with our families for Thanksgiving, find something meaningful like a saved card sent from a child, a report card, or a forgotten toy from each person's childhood, wrap it up, and "serve" on each plate.

In the end, this is one holiday that revolves around food, so no matter how you set the table, you can't miss. Happy Thanksgiving!

ℰↄ Holiday Decorations

There is nothing easier or more festive than a Christmas tree covered with hundreds of lights. I love the way the lighted tree gives the house a magical glow. You almost don't have to do another thing, but of course, we all do. Since I live on an island, a lot of the commercialism of the mainland misses us. It's easy to concentrate on the spirit of the holidays, making gifts and decorating our homes and visiting with friends and, in general, feeling a sense of community.

For all of us, wherever we live, the holidays are a time of traditions, treasures, treats, reflections, friends, and family. It's a time when many of us are moved to enrich our lives by adding to the joy or comfort of others. And, while most of us are so busy we can't imagine adding one more chore to our lives, we do it all. We make the Christmas cookies, we scour the stores for the perfect gift, we visit a sick friend, we decorate our homes, we remember family.

Keep It Simple

If you can't imagine doing anything more than throwing a few greens on the mantel or a wreath on the door, you might like to know that my favorite decorations come from putting ordinary things together or simply coming up with a new way to do the familiar. The following are some quick and easy ideas for decorating your house with greenery.

Evergreens

Don't be restricted to traditional pine boughs for fresh greens to decorate throughout the house. Mixing pine garlands with boxwood, eucalyptus, juniper, lemon leaves, and other evergreens has become increasingly popular for wreaths and other decorations.

Freshen Up

Dress up everyday household plants for the holidays by inserting sprigs of holly into the soil around the potted plants. Tie plants with French wire-rimmed or organdy ribbons in colors to match the plant flowers.

The Fabric's the Thing

Place a white lace-edged tea cloth or a pretty silk scarf over a small table and set a pretty arrangement of dried flowers and fresh greens on top. If you don't have a suitable scarf or tablecloth, use a pretty napkin or piece of fabric. It doesn't have to cover the tabletop completely. If the cloth is much larger than the table, create soft graceful folds and arrange sprigs of greens and small ornaments between them.

A Spot of Color

Fill small bowls with cranberries and popcorn and insert sprigs of holly in each. Place the bowls on a pretty platter or charger plate.

On the Mantel

Line the mantel with boughs of pine needles, and string clear lights throughout. Then decorate with fresh fruit, small ornamental toys, or tiny glass balls.

Short and Sweet

How often do you use your punch bowl? I've used mine once in the many years I've owned it, but I've now found a new use for this item. For an easy and quick centerpiece, fill a glass punch bowl with tree ornaments and stick sprigs of greenery here and there in the bowl. Surround with greens. When the holidays are over, remember the punch bowl when you need a decoration for a dinner party. You can always use it to hold stems of freesia, tulips, Queen Anne's lace, and flowers for other seasons. A small spiked holder placed in the center of the bottom will hold any arrangement.

Decorate What You Have

I once had a ceiling-high ficus tree on which I kept clear lights year-round. It always added sparkle in a corner when I didn't want to light the entire room. I no longer have the tree, so I fill a large country crock with tree branches I've spray-painted white. The branches are held in place with florist's clay on the bottom of the crock and they are covered with dancing lights. At Christmastime I pick fresh greens and sprigs of berries from trees in my yard and insert them between the branches. A friend of mine had the same idea, but her branches are left in their natural state. Both look great.

To Greet Guests

On an entryway table keep a bowl filled with lady's apples and limes and insert small sprigs of greens here and there. Do the same with an interesting salad bowl on the coffee table.

For the Kitchen

Small topiary trees made of rosemary will give off a delightful scent and you can add small red velvet bows here and there. For added decoration, rub the clay pot with a mixture of paint and glaze finish, or gold leaf it. Supplies are available in art stores and home centers.

For the Bathroom

Lavender is the most refreshing scent for the bathroom. Dried lavender is delightful in a pretty container, or tie a bunch with raffia and put it into a white creamer. Set this in a guest powder room. Put fragrant soaps in a basket lined with gold tissue, and insert a sprig of lavender or holly for a touch of Christmas.

Looking Up

Wherever you have a tall piece of furniture such as a hutch, china cabinet, tall bookshelves, space over the kitchen cabinets, or a tall bureau, use it to display a cluster of poinsettia plants in alternating colors of red, yellow, pink, and mottled.

Hurricane Plenty

Fill glass hurricane lamps or clear glass florist's vases with alternating layers of cranberries, green olives, cherries, and kumquats and top with a sprig of holly.

Door Decor

If you have large windows, French or sliding glass doors, hang sprays of greens tied with red taffeta bows down the center of the glass. Attach one end of a strip of ribbon to the top of each door or window and attach the hanging end to the back of the greens to hold in place.

How to Make a Gorgeous Garland

If you have access to evergreens it's silly to buy garlands when you can make your own. It's really easy. You'll need eight- to ten-inch-long evergreen cuttings, a package of black plastic trash bags, a large spool of florist's wire, and garden clippers.

1. Gather and wrap one end of a trash bag with florist's wire. Don't cut it.

2. To create the end of the garland, gather a handful of sprigs into a bundle, hold it onto the end of the trash bag, and continue to wrap the wire around it.

3. Using the trash bag as your form, keep adding clippings so the tops of each new layer overlap the stems of the previous layer, and spiral the wire to secure them as you go along. The evergreens should hide the wire and the plastic bag.

4. When you come to the end of a bag, overlap the end of a new one, secure it with wire, and continue to cover it with greens.

5. You can make the garland as long as you want. For example, if it's to be placed over a window, you will need less material than if you want to wind it up a banister on a staircase. When the garland is as long as you want it to be, you can wrap it with a spiral of taffeta ribbon, wire small ornaments and bells here and there, and wrap it with tiny clear lights.

Unexpected Places

I remove everything that isn't white, glass, or silver from my glass-front china cabinet at Christmastime. Then I arrange greens on the front of each shelf and run tiny clear lights under and on top of every shelf to create lighting from within. Actually, I leave the lights up all year long. Trim the front of each shelf with paper doily shelf trim to hide the lights that hang down under each shelf. When the lights are on, they shine through the doily cutouts, creating a delicate pattern. The silver and glass items sparkle inside as well. The lighting inside the cabinet creates a warm glow that is most attractive. This is an inexpensive and effective way to create subtle, indirect lighting in one area of the room. Add polished red Delicious apples on top of the greens that are spread across the top of the cabinet and more lights if desired for the holidays.

❧ Christmas Candlelight

I'm of the all-white school when it comes to candles, except at Christmastime, when I often send bayberry or cranberry candles as little gifts. As far as I'm concerned, no table is completely set, whether for company or not, without candlelight. Candlelight turns an everyday meal into a special event and is definitely a must for your holiday table.

Safe Candlelight

You can find electric candle lamps with wonderful shades in gold, hunter green, and berry-red tapestry or beaded shades. They look great lined up on a table, in a window, or scattered here and there for a spot of soft lighting.

Battery-operated candles are also wonderful and safe for window sills and areas within the reach of children. I love the idea of having low lighting and candlelight during the month of December. It makes it all the more romantic.

Personalized Gift Baskets

I put together sumptuous gift baskets to take to my party hosts, or to give to a family during the holidays. Each basket contains a fat cranberry candle, golden strands of seashell tree garlands, homemade cranberry relish, and a copy of my book, *Leslie Linsley's Quick Christmas Decorating Ideas* (St. Martin's Press).

Say "Thank You" with a Candle

There are occasions when a small gift is appropriate. Your child might give a Christmas gift to a teacher or you might want to give a "thank you" gift to someone who did you a favor. Wrap a holiday candle in cellophane and tie with a beautiful organdy bow. Attach a hand-lettered card with a narrow satin ribbon or gold cord. Gold and silver pens are available in art supply stores and they are perfect for making your holiday messages look special.

Quick and Easy Ideas with Candles

1 Place a three-branched brass candelabra in the center of the table. Use ten-inch taper candles in holiday colors.

2. Use a single taper candle and holder with a glass hurricane for a centerpiece, and surround it with evergreens and colorful tree balls. Or group three hurricane lamps together.

3. If you're having a holiday buffet, place several clear glass votive holders on the dessert table as well as on occasional tables and shelves throughout the house. Spice- or fruit-scented votives are nice in some areas.

4. A unique idea for the bathroom: Tie or pull back your shower curtain and set a votive holder on the edge of the bathtub. Put another one atop a small mirrored coaster on the sink.

5. Dress up your fireplace mantel in dramatic style by grouping brass candleholders with festive, colored, taper candles in rich red, evergreen, ivory, white, burgundy, gold or silver. I like golden pears as a mantel decoration between the candlesticks. To stay with the fruit theme, scoop out a hole, just large enough to hold a candle, in the tops of Delicious apples.

6. Add sparkle to a coffee table or side table by combining pillar candles of various heights and widths atop a decorative mirror or silver platter.

7. Place colored marbles in the bottom of a glass bowl filled with water. Then add scented floating candles.

8. Use peppermint- or spearmint-scented votives in a frosted glass votive holder.

9. Fill a terra-cotta clay pot with sand and arrange tall candles or short votives in the sand. Scatter shells or silver and gold stars over the sand for a decorative touch.

10. For a medieval look, stick brass upholstery tacks at random all around the outside of a short, fat, white candle.

ᔥ Stress-Free Christmas Decorating

It seems we all have more obligations during the holidays than at any other time of the year. Since attending two nursery and elementary school performances I've become acutely aware that most people are too busy with jobs and family to entertain or decorate lavishly. In that regard the following will give you some ideas for do-it-yourself party decorations that will make your home warm, elegant, and inviting without an inordinate amount of time invested.

No Time to Decorate
Cut large branches of pine and arrange on a mantel. Set fat candles inside hurricane lamps and place on each end of the mantel. If you don't have hurricane lamps, improvise with glass vases.

Centerpiece
Fill a large container with greens and add clear tree lights. Or fill a large basket with cut greens from your yard or garden center. If you want to add a lovely holiday scent to the house and create a festive area, fill a large wicker laundry basket (available in supermarkets for around $5) with pine branches. Scatter pinecones over the branches.

Red and Green
Wrap "pretend" packages with red, green, or silver shiny paper, tie with lavish silver ribbons or white satin, and pile on a silver tray to decorate a side table or for use as a centerpiece. The boxes can be empty, or use any boxes from the food pantry to wrap and use just for decoration. My favorites are small individual cereal boxes.

Decorate with Food
Heap ripe apples, pears, tangerines, lemons, limes, and crab apples into a bowl laced with pinecones. Even a pretty container

filled with red potatoes can be spruced up with sprigs of rosemary to decorate a table. You'll be surprised at how many compliments you'll get.

An artist friend puts small apples on wooden skewers to dress up a cooked ham or sliced turkey on the buffet table. He also does wonderful things with slices of raw vegetables by arranging them in interesting baskets. Then he adds long branches of greens picked from a backyard tree.

Light It Right

My artist friend hosts a holiday buffet every year. The table is lit with tall, fat candles he buys from a floral supply or garden center. He then drills several holes in the wood to hold the candles and covers the wood with silver foil or wrapping paper. This is then surrounded with a variety of large and interesting vegetable shapes such as a head of cabbage, a variety of squash, and whatever is appealing from the produce section. It can be a creative experience to look at food as a decorative element rather than for eating.

Creative Table Covering

I like to cover a buffet table with large leafy greens such as kale, spinach, cabbage, chard, curly lettuce, and other vegetables that I can't identify but look great. Place your serving dishes on top of the greens and arrange them so the leaves surround the plates in a pleasing way. If you can get different heights this also adds interest.

You Can't Go Wrong with Fresh Flowers

It's fun to use unusual containers for holding flowers. For example, use a wine bottle box, a mixing bowl, or a wooden salad bowl to hold delicate flowers such as roses or freesia.

Make individual floral arrangements for each guest at your dinner table. Spray-paint laurel leaves silver (or use as is), and with a glue stick attach them lengthwise so they overlap around a glass jar. Tie a pretty ribbon or cord around the center of the jar and fill each one with fresh flowers.

Candles

Candles have always played a part in Christmas celebrations. Did you know that in Iceland families light candles daily to compensate for the lack of natural light? Candles are an easy way to make us feel better, as they enhance every setting and every room. Another fact about candles: Twice as many ivory-colored candles are sold than any other shade. However, this year's candle colors are brighter than ever before with lime, orange, and yellow as the newest colors.

It doesn't cost much to buy good quality candles that burn for a long time. Beeswax, which has long been used in church candles, is enjoying renewed popularity, and many people are discovering how easy it is to make their own.

Create a Glow

For a while I lived in an apartment in New York City. We had just moved in and it was the week before Christmas. We hardly had furniture, let alone the accessories with which to create a warm and inviting holiday environment. But we wanted to have a party. So we used lots and lots of candles everywhere to create a wonderfully romantic and festive ambience. There were votives and candles on windowsills, in the bathroom, and on every surface in the living room. The kitchen counters were lined with groups of candles on trays. There was no harsh overhead lighting in the place. We had no lamps so there was no other lighting. Try this and you'll be surprised at the soft and festive glow you can create. Best of all, no one will notice what furnishings are missing or are not as nice as you'd like.

The Perfect Hostess Gift

You can never go wrong with candles and candleholders if you need a last-minute gift. Candle shades are also back in vogue, which goes back to the Victorian era. The popular item in this category is beaded-glass-and-metal-filigree shades. This is an easy item to find at a price you can afford. While there are extremely beautiful, and costly, candle lamps, you can get the look very inexpensively.

Scented Candles

Many designers have come out out with scented candles in their fragrance. These are offered in special containers like pretty glass or terra-cotta pots for gift giving. Burn scented candles only for a short period of time so the odor doesn't become overpowering. Always have unscented candles in the room as well and never use scented candles on the dining room table where food is being served.

Candles and Flowers

Many florist shops sell candles and creative holders along with flowers and foliage. In fact, some floral designers feel that candles are an integral part of any floral arrangement. At least they belong on the table right alongside the flowers.

A Fruity Solution

If you don't have interesting or pretty candleholders or if you want a new look this Christmas, make your own candleholders. Cut a hole in the top of an orange large enough to hold a votive candle and surround the cut edge with cloves.

Greeting Guests

Don't begin your decorations inside; start greeting guests with candlelight on your front porch. Surround candles in glass globes with sprigs of greenery set on the railing or steps. It's a great way to set a holiday mood.

Carry Your Style with You

And finally, if you aren't entertaining, but rather being entertained, bring along a nice bottle of wine or bubbly in a creative container. It's simple to stitch up a pretty bag from a strip of satin, velvet, or taffeta. Cut the strip so it's twice as long as the bottle plus three to four inches, and as wide as the bottle plus three to four inches. With right sides facing, fold the fabric in half lengthwise, stitch up the sides, turn right side out, fold the top edge under, stitch around, and there you have it. Slip the bottle inside, gather the fabric at the neck of the bottle, and tie with an elegant ribbon. It's so much nicer than a paper bag. Have a happy, healthy, and stress-free Christmas.

ℬ Decorating the Front Door

Decorations on the front door are the very first impressions you give to guests during the holidays. Where I live, many people hang a simple wreath or pine branches even before Thanksgiving weekend. Since the houses in town are close together and close to the street, passersby can enjoy this holiday spirit. It's easy to create a mood and feeling with anything from a few branches of greens tied with a bow to a very ornately decorated wreath. To make your own wreath, you'll find the forms and all the fixings in a well-supplied garden center. The following ideas are borrowed from my book, *Leslie Linsley's Quick Christmas Decorating Ideas* (St. Martin's Press).

Basket of Greenery

Quite by accident I discovered a delightful decoration for my front door. While searching in my basement for just the right size container to fill with greens, I came upon my bicycle basket. Flat across the back and curved in the front, it proved to be perfect for hanging on the door. I lined it with a plastic tray and filled it with branches of pine and pepperberries along with a few sprigs of holly leaves. You can also use a plastic bag to hold the arrangement inside the basket. Fill it with an inch or two of water, and the cut branches won't dry out. You can leave as is, or attach a decorative bow to the front of the basket.

Simply Stated

Tie a few pine branches together with wire and then wrap with wide, taffeta ribbon. Look for ribbon that has wired edges. I prefer deep hunter green or burgundy ribbon edged with gold. Make a fat bow. The wire edges will keep the shape of the bow intact. Cut the ends of the ribbons extra long so you have two streamers. Then ruffle them into soft ripples hanging down over the pine needles. You might like to add a few small golden glass balls here and there on the pine branches for a lovely, elegant door decoration.

A Welcome Garland

If you didn't dry your own flowers in the fall, don't despair. Dried flowers of all varieties are available at garden centers and can sometimes be found in the supermarket. It's easy to handcraft a garland from cockscomb, pink straw flowers, wheat, bay leaves, lavender, lemon leaves, rosebuds, and moss. Attach this to the front door or hang it over the fireplace mantel. To make a garland you'll need: heavy string cut to desired length of garland, green florist's tape, florist's tie wire, florist's picks, clippers, sprigs of greenery, and decorative accessories such as pinecones, pods, berries, and dried fruit.

1. Cut a bunch of greens about ten inches long. Hold them against the twine and wrap with florist's tape.

2. Continue adding and wrapping greens so each bunch overlaps the previous stems.

3. Tie wire to pinecones and attach. Use the picks to secure berries and small bunches of dried flowers. Push the picks under the green tape.

Just a Bundle

Use long cinnamon sticks and pink pepperberry to create a bundle the size of a small log. Wrap jute around the center to hold them together, and hang on the door for a fragrant and simple decoration.

Simply Stated

Bundle branches of white pine and winterberry and tie them together with raffia or a red ribbon edged with gold.

For the Cook

Create this simple door decoration. Gather a bundle of fragrant sprigs of bay leaves, rosemary, and pepper berries and tie with raffia for hanging. If you don't have an overhang or your front door isn't protected, consider using this decoration to hang in your kitchen.

Fruit and Fancy

Start with a balsam fir wreath. Then add bits and pieces of bark, twigs, slices of fruit, nuts, and leaves. You'll find these in craft stores and garden centers, if not around your own home. Secure them with florist's wire or a hot glue gun. Add a red plaid flannel bow for a different touch.

For the Birds

Use a straw ring form for the base of your wreath. You'll need florist's wire and clippers to attach twigs and branches, a raffia bow, small birdhouse, artificial birds, bundles of birdseed wrapped in gauze, and a bird's nest tucked into the twigs and branches. Fill with birdseed if you want to attract the birds.

Hydrangeas

In New England the hydrangea bushes bloom late into the fall. When dry they are wonderful for wreath-making. Depending on the soil, the blossoms can be deep or pale blue, yellowish green, pale pink, or deep cranberry. These round fat clumps of blossoms are secured to a straw or foam wreath form with florist pins so they are close together and cover the form. This is an indoor wreath since moisture will ruin it. Add a bow in a color to match the flowers and you'll have one of the prettiest displays for your windows or hallway.

Seashell Wreath

You can use any shells for this project, but deep blue mussel shells make the prettiest simple wreath. Use a flat Styrofoam or

Bristol board wreath form and hot-glue the mussel shells in concentric circles around the wreath. Add a simple bow fashioned from netting, or leave as is.

Brass Band

If you have a brass knocker on your front door, use it as part of your wreath decoration. Wire tiny golden balls to an evergreen wreath and place it on the door with the knocker in the center.

A Fanciful Display

I usually make a wreath that evolves as I go along. Last year I used a grapevine form on which I attached all sorts of miscellaneous decorations. It's good to use a hot glue gun for many such crafting projects. For this I assembled a variety of pinecones, some artificial holly leaves, and berries in different sizes, dried flowers such as rosebuds and baby's breath, small jingle bells, and several greeting cards. One of the cards featured playful mice, another had flowers and butterflies. I cut out the ones I liked best, then glued them here and there around the wreath. A mouse is perched on top of a pinecone, a butterfly rests on a dried flower. You can use small ornaments such as teddy bears, baby's blocks, a tiny Santa, and bells.

Personalized Wreath

It's easy to personalize a wreath with wooden letters. These are available in craft stores along with different wooden shapes such as candy canes, trees, stockings, stars, and hearts. Paint them with bright colors and hot-glue them around a wreath form. The letters can spell out your family name or the names of your children.

Golden Greetings

Spray-paint bay leaves with gold, then combine them with unpainted leaves to create a green and gilded wreath. With a hot glue gun, attach a layer of alternating leaves around a grapevine wreath frame, overlapping as you glue the leaves in place. Use gold-mesh French wire ribbon to make a bow for the top and allow the ends of the ribbons to stream down over the wreath. The gold and green of the leaves fairly shimmers.

Ribbon Wreath

Make a wreath entirely of ribbons for your entryway. You'll need a ten-inch heavy wire or brass ring and a fifty-yard spool of half-inch decorative ribbon. Cut the ribbon into ten-inch lengths and tie each length into a bow on the ring. Fill the ring with bows pushed together so the wreath is very full. Keep tying bows on the ring until you can no longer fit any more and the wreath is pleasingly plump.

Kumquat Wreath

A ring of kumquats and bay or lemon leaves makes a deliciously simple wreath. You'll need a twelve-inch brass or heavy wire ring, twenty-six-gauge wire, an embroidery needle, about twenty kumquats, and about forty bay or lemon leaves. Using the large-eye needle and wire, thread the kumquats (through the ends) into a circle to fit around the twelve-inch ring. Wire the leaves to the ring. Then lay the necklace of kumquats over this and wire it to the ring. Hang with a deep green ribbon.

Woodland Wreath

Start with a fir wreath from the garden shop and make it more interesting by wiring boughs of long needle pines, eucalyptus, and cedar all around. Add a wired white organdy bow to delicately top if off.

Red All Over

Start with a no-frills evergreen wreath and add your own decorations to make it personal. I usually pick up a wreath when buying my Christmas tree. Here's a simple project the kids can help with. Make wrapping paper with red and white designs and wrap small jewelry-size boxes to decorate the wreath. You can even decorate large pieces of paper in the same way to use for wrapping all your gifts. You will need: shiny white wrapping paper, red acrylic paint, a natural sponge, a pencil with a new eraser end, red and white yarn.

1. Squirt a small amount of paint onto a paper plate or into a ceramic bowl (acrylic paint is completely washable).

2. Spread the shiny paper onto a work surface, dip the sponge into the paint, dab the excess onto newsprint, then pounce the sponge up and down on the white paper to create a random pattern of texture. Set this aside to dry.

3. Spread another sheet of paper. Dip the eraser end of the pencil into the paint and then dab it onto newsprint. Cover the paper with red polka dots.

You can continue to make all sorts of wrapping paper in this way. For example, use an artist's brush to paint swirls all over one sheet, and a rubber stamp to make a repeat pattern over another. Let the paper dry, then use it to wrap small boxes. Tie each with a double strand of red and white yarn. Wire in place all around the wreath. Make a bow on the wreath with lots of red and white loops of yarn.

ɞ Holiday Food Wraps

While giving food as gifts and creating interesting wrappings isn't exactly a decorating subject, it is an extension of style. At Christmastime we are decorating our homes, wrapping gifts, and entertaining. Some people enjoy making gifts to give from their kitchen. Since many people give home-baked items at Christmastime, you might like to create interesting ways to give them. Thanksgiving at our house always includes one of my Aunt Reba's cakes so I usually double the recipe in order to get a jump on Christmas. I make miniature loaves, freeze them, and make pretty wrappings to give them as hostess gifts during the holidays.

Native Foods

Nantucket has one of the country's largest cranberry bogs and the cranberries are harvested in October. Since they're fresh only at this time of year I like to make cranberry relish to store away to give as holiday gifts. Everyone off island loves this connection to the island. Perhaps there is something special about where you live that you like sharing with others. My stepson and his wife live on a farm in Ohio. They can a wide variety of vegetables, but everyone looks forward to receiving their special salsa made from the tomatoes they grow. If you make something special at Christmastime, why not create the perfect wrapping for it? It will become a tradition and your friends will look forward to receiving it every year.

Country Wraps

If you make jams or jellies or cranberry sauce, look for attractive glass jelly jars. These are available in the supermarkets. Sometimes they have special jars at this time of year. A friend of mine who makes her own jams found rounded glass jars with sculpted fruit all around. They were the same price as the plain ones. After your jars are filled properly and sealed, cut squares of gingham with pinking shears and secure the squares over the jar lids with a rubber band. Tie a satin ribbon around the lid. Make up your own labels (use the computer to give them a custom look, or handwrite with a gold pen for a homespun look) and attach a homemade card.

Botanical Wraps

Make color copies of botanical prints or seed packets and use the paper—rather than fabric—on the top of homemade jams and jellies. The print you choose can relate to the ingredients in the homemade item. Place the printed paper over the top of the sealed jar and secure with a rubber band. Then tie with a cord. Make a small card on which you write the ingredients and give your jam a title, such as my friend did: "Tangy Tomato Sauce, made with farm-grown ingredients." Punch a hole in one corner and tie to the jar lid. For these jars, she used prints of fat, juicy tomatoes.

Bright Tins

Spray-paint a bunch of same-size cookie tins in primary colors. Then interchange the lids so you have a bright blue lid on a yellow tin and a yellow lid on a red tin. Line them with matching tissue, fill and stack two or three, then tie with a ribbon. The tins will be used long after the contents have been consumed.

Parchment-Paper Wrap

Use a paper punch to punch out an outline of snowflakes, trees, or just a border of evenly spaced holes around plain white parchment paper. Wrap your packages or use the punched paper to line a basket filled with sugar cookies. The cookies might be in the shape of Christmas trees, stars, or snowflakes outlined with white icing and sprinkled with sugar. Place the basket on a table for guests to help themselves. This will create a delightfully edible decoration. And don't forget, if you make a hole in the top of each cookie before baking, you can hang the finished cookies on the tree. Use white or gold cord. Reminder: You can make cookies any time and freeze them for Christmas giving.

ꝏ Creating a Country-Style Tree

Decorating for the holidays might begin with your tree. Ornaments can be quite costly, but it's extremely easy to make your own from a few scraps of fabric. A country theme is always warm and inviting. If you use one pattern for all the ornaments, varying the look with different fabric patterns and colors, you can make enough to cover the tree in less than a weekend, and the cost is minimal.

Patchwork Hearts

Cover your tree with stuffed patchwork hearts and then make a few more to fill with dried lavender for little sachet gifts. If you have

an old quilt that's beyond repair, this is a great way to make it last forever. Cut up the good parts to turn into tree ornaments. For new fabric, use 100 percent cotton and prewash with a little bleach and fabric softener to give it a soft, faded look that will add old-quilt character to each ornament. If you like the look of quilting, you can make these hearts with prequilted fabric available in most yard goods stores. Or you can simply make stuffed patchwork heart ornaments without the quilting.

Directions for Easy Patchwork Hearts

You'll need: a piece of colorful printed fabric and a piece of white fabric, each 8 by 12 inches; a piece of muslin, 12 by 12 inches; poly-fil stuffing; 4 inches ¼-inch satin ribbon for each ornament; tracing paper.

Directions: All measurements include ¼-inch seam allowance.

1. Measure and mark 12 squares, each 2½ by 2½ inches on the wrong side of the white fabric (3 rows of 4 squares each).
2. Draw a diagonal line through all squares.
3. With right sides facing, pin the white fabric to the same size print fabric.
4. Stitch ¼ inch on each side of the diagonal lines, through both thicknesses.
5. Cut on all solid lines. Press. You'll have 24 squares made from print and white triangles.

To make patchworks: You can arrange the squares so the triangles all go in the same direction or in different directions.

1. With right sides facing, stitch 2 squares together along one side edge. Next, join another square in the same way.
2. Make 8 rows of 3 squares each.
3. With right sides facing, stitch 2 rows together along the bottom edge. Continue to join rows in this way. Press.

To make hearts: Trace a heart shape and cut out. Note: A heart-shaped cookie cutter can be used to draw a pattern.

1. Pin the pattern to the muslin and cut 1 for each ornament.
2. Pin the pattern to the patchwork and cut 1 for each ornament.

To finish: With right sides facing, pin the patchwork top to the muslin backing piece and stitch all around, leaving the top center open for turning and stuffing.

1. Clip around seam allowance and turn right side out. Stuff firmly.
2. Fold the ribbon in half to create a hanging loop and insert the raw ends into the center of the top. Slipstitch opening closed. You might want to make a small bow and stitch or glue it at this spot.

More Decorations

For added country filler and to create a lushly decorated tree, use pinking shears to cut strips of either muslin or the fabric used for the ornaments, and tie bows on branches between the hearts. Add bundles of dried baby's breath as well.

Tree Toppers

Top the tree with a quilted angel or continue the theme by using the same patchwork method to make a large star. Simply draw a star pattern on cardboard (rounding the points rather than making them very pointy), place it on your patchwork fabric, and cut out as you did for the hearts. Just remember to add 1/4 inch extra all around when cutting out, to allow for seams when stitching. When stuffing the stars, I find the eraser end of a pencil or a crochet hook handy for getting the stuffing into each point. Happy crafting!

℘ Last-Minute Holiday Decorating Ideas (That Don't Look It!)

When my daughters were small we always made the ornaments that went on our tree. This is a good project to do with kids, and every year you add to the previous year's output. Now that my children are grown I'm always surprised when I see how laden their trees are with all the ornaments we made over the years. And they are adding their own creations, which seems like a nice tradition to have passed on. These don't have to be extravagant or difficult and you can start right now even if you've already decorated your tree. There's always room for more.

The following are some last-minute decorating ideas that are truly quick and easy and require absolutely no brain power, talent, or energy.

1. For a festive table: Stamp a design of a gold leaf pattern over a white linen tablecloth.

2. With a gold pen, draw swirls of patterns on glass balls and pile them into a glass bowl for a centerpiece. I piled my gold, bronze, and silver balls into a large pewter ashtray. A few sprigs of greens or golden strand of garlands wound here and there make a nice table decoration.

3. Wrap plants, make bows for the backs of chairs, tie back curtains with ribbon. It will dress up anything instantly.

4. Fill large glass bowls with potpourri and set votive candles in the centers. When the candle warms the inside of the bowl the scent of the potpourri is released.

5. Surround a tabletop tree with gorgeous packages wrapped with simple materials such as Kraft paper, jute, or gold mesh. I love cellophane for wrapping around colored tissue paper. Gather the ends and squinch together a few inches from the top, then tie with a pretty organdy ribbon.

6. Simple quilted wall hangings can be used for table covers and later as winter throws. There are many that are quite inexpensive.

7. No time to shop? Make a centerpiece or mantel decoration by filling a lovely bowl with green moss topped with bright golden pears. Tie an elegant bow around the bowl. If you don't have moss, use gold tissue paper.

8. For an instant holiday lift to your sofa or chairs, wrap your throw pillows with fat satin ribbons, just like a package.

9. Combine large red and gold tree ornaments with red and green apples in a bowl.

10. Place votive candles in glass tumblers and wrap each with gold mesh, organdy, or a pretty ribbon.

11. Hollow out artichokes (more unusual than apples) to hold votive candles.

12. Frame a montage of family pictures from Christmases past and hang it in the entryway or prop it up on the mantel among the greenery.

13. Put a miniature tree in the kitchen and cover with candy canes, and tie Christmas candies to the branches.

14. If you really want a minimal idea, here's what my friend Michael does for celebrations in his store. He has a large basket lined with brightly colored fabric that he fills to brimming with red and green M&M's. Put this on a table in your entryway and watch them disappear! It's festive, it's fun, and kids and adults love them.

15. Place a small electric candle lamp in the powder room and add red guest towels. Fill a small vase or pitcher with sprigs of pine or fill a basket with pinecones.

16. If you've run out of wrapping paper and there's one more gift to wrap, use the comic pages from the newspaper, a child's art-

work, leftover wallpaper, shelf paper, or magazine pages taped together in an interesting and colorful collage.

17. If you run out of name tags, simply write the recipient's name along the ribbon ends of the bow. Or use glue and short pieces of ribbon to "print" the person's name on a white gift box.

18. The prettiest ornaments can be the simplest. Dip Christmas balls into white semigloss latex enamel so the bottom half is covered with a snowlike pattern. Or sponge-paint the white enamel at random over red and green balls. This is a fun project to do with kids. Dip pinecones into the paint and hang as little snow-covered trees on the larger tree. While the paint is still wet, sprinkle the pinecones with glitter if desired.

19. For a no-effort decoration, tie tiny sprigs of greens together and hang them upside down from windowpanes. Gather a large bunch of greens, tie with white satin ribbon, and affix to one top corner of the window frame.

20. Finally, there's nothing fresher or more Christmasy than greens picked from the backyard. Simply lay them across the mantel, over a sideboard, along the top of the kitchen cabinets. Then add a string of clear lights and your house will exude a festive feeling with the least bit of effort.

Index